Benjamin Franklin

Titles in the series Critical Lives present the work of leading cultural figures of the modern period. Each book explores the life of the artist, writer, philosopher or architect in question and relates it to their major works.

In the same series

Benjamin Franklin

Kevin J. Hayes

REAKTION BOOKS

For Tom Barden

Published by
REAKTION BOOKS LTD
Unit 32, Waterside
44–48 Wharf Road
London N1 7UX, UK
www.reaktionbooks.co.uk

First published 2022
Copyright © Kevin J. Hayes 2022

Printed and bound in Great Britain by Bell & Bain, Glasgow

A catalogue record for this book is available from the British Library

ISBN 978 1 78914 517 5

Contents

Benjamin Franklin: The Statesman and Philosopher, 1847, lithograph.

Introduction

Benjamin Franklin casts a long shadow. In 1870, eighty years after Franklin's death, Mark Twain wrote 'The Late Benjamin Franklin'. With its homey epigraph, Twain's essay reflects the lasting power of the saws and sayings from *Poor Richard's Almanack*. Instead of repeating what Franklin says about procrastination – 'Never leave that till tomorrow which you can do today' – Twain spoofs it: 'Never put off till tomorrow what you can do day after tomorrow just as well.'[1]

Poor Richardisms focus Twain's facetiousness. Franklin, he says, 'prostituted his talents to the invention of maxims and aphorisms calculated to inflict suffering upon the rising generation of all subsequent ages'. He made life hell for boys. Whenever one tried squeezing some pleasure from life, his father would throw Franklin in his face.[2]

Many have read Twain's essay as a complaint, but J. A. Leo Lemay reads it as a compliment, a playful homage by a fellow journalist, printer, humourist and maxim-monger. Twain's biography supports Lemay's interpretation. His brother Orion Clemens reprinted several Poor Richardisms in his Missouri newspaper and named his Iowa printing house the Ben Franklin Book and Job Office. As his brother's apprentice, Twain followed Franklin, who apprenticed in his brother James's Boston printing house. Travelling to Philadelphia in 1853, Twain visited Franklin's tomb and toured Independence Hall, where he deliberately sat where Franklin had sat. Three years later, Twain delivered a speech commemorating Franklin's 150th birthday. And two decades after that, Twain reread and annotated Franklin's autobiography.[3]

Franklin's is the most famous autobiography in American literature. Its episodes have become familiar to readers around the globe, especially the story of Benjamin breaking his indenture, going on the lam to escape his brother's abuse and reaching Philadelphia, where he found himself munching a puffy roll while carrying others as he toured the city on a long day that ended at the Crooked Billet Tavern. Franklin takes his personal story through his electrical experiments to his 1757 journey to London, where it cuts off, leaving unwritten his legislative, diplomatic and literary life during the Revolutionary era.

The weight that Twain gives to Franklin's famous sayings compared to the autobiography reflects how influential they had become. But it was not *Poor Richard's* per se that immortalized the maxims, but one particular part of one particular almanac. *Poor Richard's Almanack* for 1758, Franklin's last, included 'Father Abraham's Speech', a 'greatest hits' compilation from his earlier almanacs. Speaking to some bargain-hunters, Father Abraham repeats numerous Poor Richardisms, telling the crowd, 'Let us hearken to good advice, and something may be done for us; "God helps them that help themselves," as Poor Richard says.'[4]

The next year Franklin's nephew, namesake and quondam printing partner Benjamin Mecom separately issued *Father Abraham's Speech*, which would reappear countless times as *The Way to Wealth*, a title that puffs it as a self-help guide to money-making. *The Way to Wealth* became a staple of the chapmen's trade. Travelling salesmen known as chapmen would fill their packs with little books known as chapbooks and sell them across the countryside. As a chapbook, *The Way to Wealth* permeated America. It widely disseminated Franklin's famous sayings and crystallized his reputation as the Wizard of Saws. With a three-decade head start on the autobiography, *The Way to Wealth* also conditioned how people perceived Franklin's life.

Reprints were not restricted to America. During the eighteenth century *The Way to Wealth* was translated into French, Gaelic, German, Italian and Russian. One London printer issued *The Way to Wealth* in 1779 as a broadside, a one-page edition suitable for framing. English publishers from Bath to Canterbury subsequently reissued more broadsides. Perhaps Twain's account is not so hyperbolic. Hanging a framed copy of *The Way to Wealth* in the parlour, parents could remind their children daily about Franklin's wisdom.[5]

The French traveller Michel Chevalier, who visited Cincinnati, Ohio, in 1834, was impressed by how the city had grown. Its founders had 'brought with them nothing but sharp-sighted, wakeful, untiring industry', Chevalier observed. 'They seem to have chosen Franklin for their patron-saint, and to have adopted Poor Richard's maxims as a fifth gospel.' The history of publishing confirms Chevalier's observation. One Cincinnati publisher reprinted *The Way to Wealth* in 1815.[6] With little more than Franklin's admonition to hard work, Ohio settlers created Cincinnati. *The Way to Wealth* settled the West.

Franklin's pamphlet is closely connected to Chevalier's Saint-Simonist philosophy. Claude Henri de Rouvroy, Comte de Saint-Simon, believed industrial leaders should control society to encourage hard work and eliminate poverty. Saint-Simon foresaw a world based not on wealth or privilege but on merit. Studying with Jean le Rond d'Alembert, he learned about science. Fighting on the American side during the War of Independence, he learned about hard work. Saint-Simon believed that together, science and industry could accelerate civilization. He deeply respected America's Founding Fathers. Franklin, for one, united the labourer's persistence, the philosopher's sagacity and the scientist's patience.[7]

In his preface to a French edition of *The Way to Wealth*, Chevalier calls Franklin 'a worker who became a great statesman and a great philosopher'. His preface closes with a saying loosely adapted from Franklin's 'Advice to a Young Tradesman', which the pamphlet's cover repeats: 'If anyone says you can get rich by some means besides industry and frugality, then do not listen to him; he is a viper.'[8]

Diligent nineteenth-century readers went beyond *The Way to Wealth* and the autobiography. Honoré de Balzac, who appreciated Franklin as scientist, writer and statesman, quipped, 'His legacy is the lightning rod, the hoax and the republic.'[9] Before Balzac, Lord Byron had said something similar. Byron enjoyed Franklin's hoax 'Parable against Persecution', which he called a 'beautiful moral parable in favour of toleration'.[10] He paid homage to Franklin's electrical research and revolutionary politics in 'The Age of Bronze':

> Franklin's quiet memory climbs to heaven,
> Calming the lightning which he thence hath riven,
> Or drawing from the no less kindled earth
> Freedom and peace to that which boasts his birth.[11]

Byron's friend Leigh Hunt lacked his enthusiasm. He called *Poor Richard's Almanack* 'a heap of "scoundrel maxims"', borrowing a phrase from James Thomson's *Castle of Indolence*. Describing a miser, Thomson says, 'A penny saved is a penny got,/ Firm to this scoundrel maxim keepeth he.' Hunt assumed all Franklin's aphorisms concerned getting and spending. They might befit a rising commercial nation, Hunt said, but the Old World could do without them.[12]

Since liberal politics shaped Hunt's journalism, his animosity towards Franklin – 'the greatest liberalizing force in eighteenth-century America', Stuart P. Sherman would say – is all the more enigmatic.[13] Hunt acknowledged Franklin's role in extending the sphere of liberty but disavowed his crass American commercialism.

Hunt would recycle his earlier Franklin discussion in his own autobiography, prefacing it with an unfair, but vivid comment:

> I cannot get it out of my head that the Americans are Englishmen with the poetry and romance taken out of them; and that there is one great counter built along their coast from north to south, behind which they are all standing like so many linendrapers.[14]

One Irish reviewer corrected him, emphasizing Franklin's kind-hearted benevolence to show that Hunt 'wholly mistakes the character of the man'.[15]

During his lifetime, Franklin became known for his anecdotes as well as his aphorisms. Samuel Johnson had James Boswell to record his wit and wisdom; Franklin made everyone a Boswell. Friends recorded his anecdotes for posterity. Surviving through the nineteenth century, they (the anecdotes, not the friends) form a major contribution to the history of American humour. They bolster Franklin's popular image as an American folk hero, a wise sage who derived moral lessons from everyday life.

According to one traditional story, Benjamin's father Josiah Franklin used to say a lengthy grace before meals, a habit Benjamin despised. While Josiah salted their winter provisions one day, Benjamin told him he could save time by saying grace over the whole cask. It seems unlikely that Benjamin actually said these words to his churchgoing father, but the anecdote stuck.[16]

This episode resurfaced in the early twentieth century with the rise of Taylorism, a social movement not dissimilar to Saint-Simonism. Based on Frederick Winslow Taylor's thought, Taylorism positions the industrial engineer as a social manager who makes the world more efficient. Repeating the anecdote, one Taylorist magazine called Franklin 'the first efficiency expert'.[17]

The year 1906 marked the bicentenary of Franklin's birth. Albert Henry Smyth got a head start, issuing the early volumes of his edition of Franklin's writings the previous year. Sherman said of Smyth's edition, 'The Franklin now discoverable in the ten volumes of his complete works is one of the most widely and thoroughly cultivated men of his age.'[18] The edition was not exactly complete. Disliking what he called Franklin's 'salt imagination' – a phrase from *Measure for Measure* – the prudish Smyth omitted his funniest stuff:

> His humour is coarse and his mood of mind Rabelaisian. His 'salt imagination' delights in greasy jests and tales of bawdry. He came of a grimy race of hard-handed blacksmiths, and they had set their mark on him. With all his astonishing quickness and acuteness of intellect and his marvellous faculty of adaptation, he remained to the end of life the proletarian, taking an unclean pleasure in rude speech and coarse innuendo.[19]

A vast amount of scholarship has followed Smyth's edition, but Franklin's bawdy humour has rarely received the serious study it deserves. Popular culture has filled the gap. Asserting that the world's greatest geniuses secretly write its best dirty jokes, Mark Hentemann named several authors for proof, starting with Franklin.[20]

In 1917 the initial volume of *The Cambridge History of American Literature* appeared. Carl Van Doren had invited Sherman – his teacher – to co-edit this collaborative history and assigned to him the Franklin chapter, a task Sherman thoroughly enjoyed. Sherman privately told Van Doren that Franklin was the 'richest subject I have touched for a long time. Day and night I quote Franklin.'[21]

Franklin excelled as a civic leader, diplomat, inventor, politician, publisher and scientist. Reducing him to a spinner of homespun wisdom, Sherman argued, diminishes his achievement. Franklin also encouraged others to pursue their scientific, literary and political goals. Ultimately, he may be recognized more for the impetus he gave others. Sherman expressed this idea with a dynamic metaphor: 'His mind was a teeming warren of hints and suggestions. He loved rather to start than to pursue the hare.'[22]

Challenging Franklin's lofty historical stature in *Studies in Classic American Literature*, D. H. Lawrence paradoxically reinforced it. Lawrence's Franklin chapter is well known, but he wrote an earlier version that is not. Using Taylorist language, Lawrence argued that Franklin conceived God as 'an efficient manager' who 'sees that the business of the universe – that great and complicated factory of revolving worlds – is kept profitably going'.[23]

Lawrence's Franklin recalls Mary Shelley's *Frankenstein*. In *The Frankenstein Notebooks*, Charles E. Robinson says that Shelley deliberately named her monster-making scientist to conjure up the spectre of Benjamin Franklin. Lawrence went Mary Shelley one better. She implicitly compared Dr Franklin with Dr Frankenstein; Lawrence explicitly compared Franklin with Frankenstein's monster. His regimented scheme for achieving moral perfection made the construction of the individual akin to the monster's unnatural creation. The thirteen moral virtues Franklin describes in his autobiography are his components. By perfecting and assembling them, he made himself the ideal man, 'a virtuous Frankenstein monster'.[24]

Rewriting his earlier version for *Studies in Classic American Literature* while living in Taos, New Mexico, Lawrence Americanized his text, capturing the local patois. To Sherman's eyes, Lawrence's Franklin chapter resembled a Keystone comedy: 'Clapping that sturdy storekeeper, Benjamin Franklin, on the back and twirling him around with many a shrewd punch in the midriff, [Lawrence] explains just why he doesn't care for the "old scout".'[25]

Lawrence dropped the comparison with Frankenstein's monster as he revised. American imagery worked better, he decided. The Franklin chapter begins, 'The perfectibility of man! Ah heaven, what a dreary theme! The perfectibility of the Ford car!'[26] Lawrence also traded the general comment about Franklin's God as an efficient factory manager for specific examples such as John Wanamaker, whose grand department stores bore his name and manifested his retail philosophy. Lawrence observed, 'God is the supreme servant of men who want to get on, to produce. Providence. The provider. The heavenly store-keeper. The everlasting Wanamaker.'[27]

While compelled to consider Lawrence's ideas, subsequent observers have often dismissed them. V. S. Pritchett said Lawrence could not hold a candle to Franklin: 'Before Franklin's irony, urbanity and benevolence, Lawrence cuts an absurd figure, rather like a Sunday School teacher who has gone to a social dressed up as a howling dervish, when fancy dress was not requested.'[28]

Starting 'The Pursuit of Happiness' with Lawrence's 'everlasting Wanamaker', D. W. Brogan offered an alternative interpretation. He viewed Franklin's modernity as something positive. He was 'a prophet and a maker of the modern world of machinery, science, law and order which Lawrence despised'. Writing in 1939, the year Britain entered the Second World War, Brogan saw Franklin as a culture hero. With Hitler's rise to power, people longed for the world Franklin and the other Founding Fathers created, a world 'in which "life, liberty and the pursuit of happiness" could be proclaimed as the axiomatic subjects of the State'.[29]

Brogan's essay reviews Carl Van Doren's eight-hundred-page biography. A *rara avis*, Van Doren's *Benjamin Franklin* is a scholarly work with mass appeal. The biography remains readable, though it sometimes seems quaint. Van Doren takes Franklin's autobiography and other writings as gospel and quotes big chunks without question. To his credit, Van Doren does question anecdotes from outside Franklin's writings.

One story reports something that Franklin supposedly said when he and fellow delegates to the Continental Congress signed the Declaration of Independence. After John Hancock said, 'We must be unanimous; there must be no pulling different ways; we must all hang together,' Franklin replied, 'We must indeed all hang together, or most assuredly we shall all hang separately.' Franklin could have spoken these characteristic words, but Van Doren could not locate the anecdote before its appearance in Jared Sparks's 1840 edition of Franklin's writings.[30]

Hitherto unrecorded evidence complicates matters. Widely reprinted during the late 1830s, this anecdote stems from an article in the New York *Evening Post* that appeared in 1836. The phrase itself was around decades earlier. In his 1801 play *Life, A Comedy* Frederick Reynolds has Mr Craftly say, 'As the joke goes, if we don't hang together, by Heavens we shall hang separately.'[31]

Franklin could have initiated the joke or, faced with the possibility that the failure of their rebellion would result in their execution, he could have repeated a current phrase. Franklin's joke, if it is Franklin's joke, reflects a tradition in American humour, which turns dark when goings get rough. While questioning its veracity, Van Doren could not expunge the anecdote. It was so vital to the Franklin legend that it would keep being repeated. Despite its dark humour, it forms a statement of principle, expressing the American revolutionaries' willingness to risk life for liberty.

Van Doren's biography was warmly received. Perhaps no reviewer understood Franklin's literary talent better than Malcolm Cowley, who could see why Franklin excelled as a writer:

> He applied the theory of the Mask, as it would later
> be expressed by William Butler Yeats. That is, a great
> man may overcome his weaknesses and redouble his
> influence by creating a false character for himself, based
> on exactly those qualities in which he is lacking.[32]

Franklin did not wear one mask: he wore many. In the 'Silence Dogood' essays, his first set of published writings and, indeed, the first essay series in American literature, he assumes the persona of a well-intended Boston widow who keeps an eagle eye on her neighbours to correct their faults.

Before finishing the series, Franklin experimented with different voices and narrative strategies. The fifth number of 'Silence Dogood' includes a letter by 'Ephraim Censorious' recommending that Silence should correct women first: 'When you have once reformed the women, you will find it a much easier task to reform the men, because women are the prime causes of a great many male enormities.'[33] The word 'enormity', which commonly meant a moral transgression, at the time could also mean something of excessive size. Modified by the adjective 'male', enormity becomes a double entendre. Franklin's bawdy joke turns 'Silence Dogood, No. 5' into a figurative matryoshka doll. He embeds the joke within a double entendre, which is embedded within Censorious's letter, thus making Censorious a dupe by having him voice the joke unwittingly. Putting Censorious's letter within Silence Dogood's, Franklin makes her complicit in the transmission of the bawdy joke.

The eighth number of 'Silence Dogood' defends freedom of speech, a defence motivated by James Franklin's imprisonment for a newspaper report that implied collusion between Massachusetts authorities and some pirates. Instead of writing an original essay, which could have been actionable, Benjamin quoted an anonymous essay by John Trenchard and Thomas Gordon from the *London Journal*. The essay would subsequently appear in *Cato's Letters*, the breviary of freedom.

The quotation begins, 'Without freedom of thought, there can be no such thing as wisdom; and no such thing as public liberty, without freedom of speech.'[34] Quoting these words, Franklin made them his own. They are inscribed in the u.s. Capitol on the first floor corridor leading to the House of Representatives. Would that current legislators would pause to read them.

Franklin invented personae with colourful names, including Abigail Twitterfield and Timothy Wagstaff, to take for example two identities he used in the *New-England Courant* to defy the stodgy values of Puritan New England. Commentators have erred by equating Franklin with Poor Richard – his most renowned persona – but Franklin invented new identities for new situations. His contributions to the London press during the Revolutionary era are especially tricky. To assert American rights, he selected identities representing his birthplace: 'Americanus', 'Homespun', 'New England'. Other times he voiced a conciliatory tone, speaking as 'Pacificus' or 'A Friend to Both Countries'. Historians sometimes misconstrue the opinions of Franklin's personae for his own.

Many writers have felt Franklin's influence. To escape notice while travelling, Hunter S. Thompson, for instance, would register at hotels under Franklin's name. When *The Guardian* asked Thompson which historical figure he identified with most closely, he replied, 'Benjamin Franklin, coz he loved electricity.' Reporting on the Watergate hearings, Thompson said that President Nixon withheld evidence from Congress to keep his henchmen from talking and himself from impeachment. He closes with a familiar saying: 'Hang together or hang separately.'[35]

In Thompson's hands the phrase attributed to Franklin acquires considerable irony. These words form a statement of principle in the Franklin anecdote; they become sneaky and underhanded when applied to a corrupt president under pressure of impeachment. They are words for a president running scared, one who coerces his staff to save himself.

Mark Twain's essay 'The Late Benjamin Franklin' has become well known. Jorge Luis Borges cited it while discussing Franklin. Thompson apparently knew it, too. Twain's *Letters from Hawaii*, which gave Thompson an epigraph for *The Curse of Lono*, says that the great Hawaiian god Lono was 'deified for meritorious services – just our own fashion of rewarding heroes, with the difference that we would have made him a postmaster instead of a god'. Speaking about heroes, Twain evokes the image of the most famous postmaster in American history, Benjamin Franklin. Evoking Twain, Thompson puts himself in a literary double play: Franklin to Twain to Thompson.[36]

Thompson's affinity for Franklin is understandable. The leading journalist of his day, Franklin innovated newspaper reporting. Thompson was a leader of New Journalism, an innovative approach to reportage. Both used fiction to enhance their journalism. Franklin wrote under many different personae; Thompson wrote his greatest work, *Fear and Loathing in Las Vegas: A Savage Journey to the Heart of the American Dream*, as Raoul Duke, a persona letting him report the truth but shade into fiction. After receiving an honorary doctorate for his electrical research, Franklin started calling himself Dr Franklin. Thompson obtained a mail order Doctor of Divinity and used his real name to shape his fictional persona, Dr Hunter S. Thompson. For both Franklin and Thompson, creating literary personae was akin to self-mythologizing. The myth-making that has taken place since Franklin's death follows a trajectory that Franklin himself started during his life.

1

The Cabinet of Curiosities

In June 1725 Sir Hans Sloane received an unusual letter. It was signed 'Benjamin Franklin', someone he did not know. Social custom deemed that one man should not introduce himself to another, but Franklin defied etiquette to write this letter, which begins, 'Having lately been in the northern parts of America, I have brought from thence a purse made of the stone asbestos.' Franklin described some other pertinent curiosities in his possession, asked if Sloane wished to buy them and said to contact him at the Golden Fan in Little Britain.[1]

Franklin was nineteen years old when he wrote this letter. For six months he had been living in London and working as a journeyman printer. Nowhere does the letter mention his age or position. Instead, it projects an air of urbanity. Though this is Franklin's earliest surviving letter, by the time he wrote it, he was already an accomplished author, having honed his literary skills by writing newspaper articles. A quick glance at his boyhood years can help put the letter to Sloane in context.

Benjamin Franklin was born in Boston, Massachusetts, on 17 January 1706, according to the new-style calendar. He was the youngest son of Josiah Franklin, a tallow chandler, and Abiah Folger Franklin. Benjamin displayed an early aptitude for reading. Family tradition says he read the Bible when he was five. Josiah Franklin had apprenticed his other sons in the trades, but in 1714 he sent Benjamin to South Grammar School to obtain a good classical education that would prepare him to enter Harvard College, where he could study for the ministry.

After one school year, Josiah Franklin pulled his son from South Grammar, partly because of its expense but also because of his growing uncertainty about the value of a Harvard education. Instead, Josiah enrolled Benjamin in George Brownell's school, where Benjamin learned writing, mathematics, music and dance. After a year, Josiah took him from Brownell's school and put him to work in his tallow chandlery. If he did not rebel soon, Benjamin feared that he would be stuck making soap and candles all his life. After he threatened to run away to sea, his father agreed to apprentice him at the printing house run by Benjamin's older brother, James.

James Franklin worked his little brother hard, but Benjamin still managed to find time to read during his apprenticeship. James had an excellent library in his printing office, which exposed Benjamin to some of the finest English writers, from William Shakespeare to Sir Richard Steele. Plays, poetry, essays, travelogues, histories: Franklin read all types of literature growing up.

The *New-England Courant*, the newspaper that James edited and published, gave Benjamin a good opportunity to improve his literary skills. A group of James's friends, who became known as the Couranteers, gathered almost daily at the printing house. Bright and witty, they contributed many fine essays to the *Courant*. Reading their articles while setting them in type and again while proofreading, Benjamin learned them well. The Couranteers excelled at the use of literary personae, and Boston readers enjoyed their clever fictional identities. The Couranteers profoundly shaped Benjamin's literary style.

When he was sixteen, Benjamin started writing for the *Courant*. The pseudonymous essays that he wrote for the newspaper demonstrate his mastery of literary personae. The ease with which he changed identities from one essay to another also reflects a central aspect of the American character. The ability of Americans to shape-shift, to remake themselves anew, has become a defining national trait. Few symbolize this impulse better than Benjamin Franklin.

Silence Dogood is his most well-known *Courant* persona, but Franklin also wrote as Hugo Grim, Silence Dogood's greatest fan, who presents Franklin's view of nascent celebrity culture; Dingo, the first African American persona in American journalism; and Jethro Standfast, a mock illiterate persona, a type of narrator that would recur numerous times throughout American literature.[2]

Franklin's use of personae carried over from his public to his private writings. As a letter writer, he would shape his voice to suit whomever he was addressing. The letter to Sloane is not only Franklin's earliest surviving letter, it is also the earliest example of how he used personae in his correspondence. While possessing the same name as its author, the 'Benjamin Franklin' who signs the letter to Sloane is also a persona, a world traveller who shares Sloane's scientific interests and gentlemanly bearing.

Franklin's audacious postscript develops his persona further: 'I expect to be out of town in 2 or 3 days, and therefore beg an immediate answer.' Instead of assuming a subservient manner as might be expected when a journeyman addresses a distinguished physician, collector and baronet, Franklin appears as an equal. A man on a tight schedule, he will be leaving London soon, perhaps for another exotic locale, and demands an answer. His letter forces its prestigious recipient to adjust his schedule to suit. After Franklin established himself as one of Philadelphia's leading citizens years later, he would again use his own name as a persona. Instead of projecting a gentlemanly identity, he would assume the persona of an artisan: 'B. Franklin, Printer'.

The letter to Sloane also reveals an incidental fact: where Franklin lived in London. The Golden Fan was a fan shop that rented upstairs rooms to lodgers. The genetic text of the autobiography, which reveals what Franklin added and subtracted in revision, provides independent verification. Drafting his manuscript, he wrote a simple declarative sentence about where he lived in London. He subsequently added two prepositional phrases to pinpoint the spot: 'at a fan shop in Little Britain'.[3]

Franklin's revisions show how carefully he crafted his personal narrative. After inserting these two phrases, he considered their symbolic resonance. 'Fan shop' sounded too frivolous, or too feminine, so he cancelled the first prepositional phrase. By mentioning Little Britain – a mecca for book lovers – he reinforced a motif that runs through his autobiography: the importance of books and reading to his life.

Flashback to Boston, September 1723: tired of his brother James's mistreatment, Benjamin Franklin devised a clever ruse to escape. A friend told the skipper of the New York sloop *Speedwell* that Franklin got a girl pregnant and had to leave town before being forced to marry her. For a fee, the captain would take him to New York. Having accumulated a substantial library, Franklin sold some books to afford his escape. He was safely aboard when the *Speedwell* left Boston Harbor.[4]

In New York, Franklin approached William Bradford for a job. The city's only printer, Bradford had nothing to offer but sent him south to Philadelphia, where his son Andrew might have work. Crossing New York Harbor in an open boat, Franklin and his fellow travellers encountered an unexpected squall, which tore the decrepit sails to pieces. They spent the stormy night on the water, a bottle of rum their only sustenance. With nary a ho-ho-ho, they passed around the bottle until it was dry, the only thing that was dry that night. Franklin came ashore burning with fever, but he recovered quickly and walked across New Jersey to the Delaware River, which took him to Market Street Wharf in Philadelphia.

Andrew Bradford, editor and publisher of the *American Weekly Mercury*, had no full-time work but gave him a place to stay until he found a job. Franklin approached Philadelphia's other printer, Samuel Keimer, who had left London and his wife the previous year. An 'odd fish', Keimer had an odd appearance to boot. He wore a long, straggly beard, which he refused to trim, citing Leviticus for support: 'Ye shall not mar the corners of thy beard.' Keimer was a compositor; he hired Franklin to man his press.[5]

One day Sir William Keith, the Pennsylvania governor, entered the shop. To Keimer's chagrin, Keith, having heard Keimer had a bright new journeyman, asked to speak with his teenaged employee, whom he invited to a nearby tavern for some madeira, a heavy wine that made one light as a grasshopper. Seeing Franklin as a potential ally, Keith encouraged him to start his own printing house. With a printer on his side, Keith would have a platform for his policies.

London was central to Keith's plans for Franklin's future. There he could obtain a printing press, type and paper. Keith promised to write letters of introduction to London friends and a letter of credit sufficient for the supplies necessary to establish a Philadelphia printing house. Franklin accepted Keith's offer but otherwise kept mum about their business plans.

If Franklin had any regrets about going to London, they concerned Deborah Read. A feisty young woman with a strong heart and stronger opinions, Deborah lived with her parents on Market Street next door to Keimer's printing house. As they grew close, Benjamin and Deborah considered making their relationship permanent, but they had settled nothing definite before he left for London.[6]

Franklin bought passage aboard Captain John Annis's *London Hope*, which had been making the Philadelphia-to-London run for years. James Ralph, a friend with literary ambitions, would accompany him. Since Ralph's young wife had recently given birth to their daughter Mary, Franklin found it strange that Ralph would take a lengthy overseas trip, but he did not pry. No passenger would be more important to Franklin than Thomas Denham, a merchant from Bristol, England, who had emigrated to Philadelphia, where he had established a successful mercantile trade.

Sadly, Annis died before their departure, so his son Thomas took command, making this his maiden voyage as captain. His men inspired little confidence. One crew member who was Franklin's age looked like a ghost: fair skinned, almost albinistic, he had white eyebrows and curly, sandy-coloured hair. Another was positively gruesome. A short, stocky, bald man, he had rotten teeth and lips so blubbery he could scarcely keep them closed. A rheum or some kind of watery discharge continually streamed from his mouth.[7]

The *London Hope* sailed in early November 1724. Rough seas challenged its new skipper, but Thomas Annis safely reached London on Christmas Eve. From Philadelphia, population 10,000, Franklin and Ralph now found themselves in a city of 700,000. Keith never did write the promised letters, so Franklin was stranded, his business plans a shambles. The width of the Atlantic separated him from home, and he lacked the funds to return. He approached Denham, revealed Keith's reneged promise and asked for advice. Denham laughed at the thought of Keith as a financier. A notorious spendthrift, Keith could give no credit because he had no credit to give.

Denham told Franklin to find a position with a London printing house, which would provide invaluable experience he could use upon returning home: an appealing idea. Without credit, Franklin could not raise sufficient capital to buy the equipment he needed. Denham offered a new way to view his plight. Knowledge could be a kind of capital. What Franklin learned as a printer in London would give him the expertise to establish his own printing house in Philadelphia.

Franklin and Ralph headed for Bartholomew Close, just north of St Paul's Cathedral, where several printers operated. Their search for nearby lodgings took them to Little Britain, a narrow

Canaletto, *St Paul's Cathedral*, *c*. 1754, oil on canvas. Searching for work as a journeyman printer in London, Franklin headed for Bartholomew Close, an area just north of St Paul's. James Ralph, who accompanied him, captured their reaction in *A Critical Review of the Publick Buildings, Statutes and Ornaments in, and about London and Westminster* (1734), p. 17: 'The grand cathedral of St. Paul's is undoubtedly one of the most magnificent modern buildings in Europe . . . The dome is without question a very stupendous fabrick, and strikes the eye with an astonishing pleasure.'

lane just off Aldersgate Street, hard by St Botolph's Church, that contained many booksellers specializing in used and rare books. The Green Dragon, John Wilcox's bookshop, was adjacent to the Golden Fan. Since Wilcox had a huge stock of second-hand books, Franklin asked to borrow individual volumes for a small fee. Wilcox agreed. With minimal expense, Franklin resumed the rigorous self-education he had begun in Boston. While living in London, he borrowed dozens of books from Wilcox.[8]

Franklin found work with Samuel Palmer, who ran his printing house from the converted Lady Chapel of the Church of

Saint Bartholomew-the-Great in Smithfield, a house of worship transformed into a place of enlightenment. Palmer's printing room was impressive. As a former chapel, it had a high ceiling with large windows all around, which admitted great shafts of light.[9]

Ralph had more trouble finding work. For the time being, Franklin's salary sufficed for them both. Personal economy came easily to Franklin. Before saying things about saving pennies, he learned to tighten his belt. He would tell dietary researcher Dr William Stark that while a journeyman printer, he 'lived a fortnight on bread and water, at the rate of ten pounds of bread per week, and that he found himself stout and hearty with this diet.'[10]

Franklin was not the only one who had lugged a secret across the Atlantic. Whereas Franklin had masked his business plans, Ralph had been keeping a darker and more disturbing secret: he had permanently abandoned his wife and daughter. Shocked by Ralph's selfishness, Franklin nonetheless remained his friend. They enjoyed the city together, often attending the theatre. Franklin would dedicate to Ralph *A Dissertation on Liberty and Necessity*, a bold philosophical pamphlet that tackled free will, human nature and good versus evil: heady stuff for a nineteen-year-old. By the time he finished his argument, Franklin had reduced personal motivation to a balance between pleasure and pain.[11]

Ralph and Franklin rented one apartment above the Golden Fan. 'Mrs T', a young milliner, rented another, so Franklin says in his autobiography. It may seem unusual that she lived by herself, but there is an easy explanation: she didn't. The paragraph introducing Mrs T in the final version of the autobiography begins, 'In our house there lodg'd a young woman,' but the genetic text reveals that Franklin initially wrote, 'In the house with us there lodg'd two single women.'[12] In revision, he combined the two women into one character. As he presents her in his final version, Mrs T is a composite created for rhetorical and didactic purposes. The version of Mrs T in the first draft may more accurately portray the real woman.

The genetic text provides enough details about Mrs T to reconstruct her circumstances. Considering her title, some biographers have assumed she was a widow, but 'Mrs' carried no marital connotations in Franklin's day. An abbreviation for 'Mistress', it often designated a female shop owner.[13] Since Mrs T owned a millinery shop, her title is appropriate. One biographer calls her 'a pleasant but poor young milliner': a sentimental cliché.[14] Franklin's account of her socio-economic status is more accurate. Describing Mrs T as 'genteelly bred', he indicated that her parents were fairly prosperous. Like other skilled trades, millinery required a lengthy apprenticeship, which could be a major investment for a family.

Eleanor Mosley, a contemporary milliner, provides a good parallel. Her parents paid £50 for Eleanor's millinery apprenticeship. By the time Franklin met Mrs T, she had completed her seven-year apprenticeship and worked as a journeywoman milliner. To trade within the City of London, women, like men, needed the freedom of the city, which required membership in a livery company. Not until Mrs T obtained both the freedom of the city and membership in a company could she have opened her shop.[15]

Establishing a millinery shop in eighteenth-century London involved a substantial investment, a capital outlay of around £400. Like Mosley's, Mrs T's parents would have invested a considerable sum to establish their daughter's business. She opened her shop in the Cloisters. A shopping centre named after its former use as the ancient monastic cloisters of St Bartholomew's, the Cloisters, one could say, let the money changers back into the temple.

As a place where money changed hands, the Cloisters was a danger zone. In *Colonel Jack*, Daniel Defoe has his hero steal a sack of money from a country gentleman at Cloister Gate. The danger Mrs T faced was closer to home. In the evenings at the Golden Fan, the smooth-talking Ralph would read plays to her, and the two grew close. Mrs T soon found out she was pregnant with Ralph's child: another fact Franklin obscured as he revised the autobiography.

Franklin's final version describes the infant as 'her child', a description that has prompted previous biographers to heap presumption atop assumption. The 'Mrs' let them assume that she was a widow; presumably, the child was the issue of Mrs T and her now-deceased husband. But Franklin's autobiography never puts the baby at the Golden Fan. The genetic text clarifies the child's paternity. Referring to Ralph, Franklin originally wrote 'his child'. Only later did he cancel the male possessive pronoun and substitute the female pronoun. In revision 'his child' became 'her child'.[16]

Ralph was Mrs T's downfall. The two left Little Britain for other lodgings. Since she was an enterprising businesswoman, Ralph assumed that they could live on the proceeds of her millinery shop while he wrote poetry. As a young, unwed mother running her own business, Mrs T had a tough go of it. Because of Ralph, she lost her friends and her business. Consequently, she lost the investment her family had made in the millinery shop.

Going to Berkshire, where he had taken a teaching position, Ralph temporarily left Mrs T in London. Ideally, he would earn enough to let her join him. To go incognito, Ralph took the name 'Benjamin Franklin', adding identity fraud to his list of transgressions. Ralph's dream of poetic fame was hopelessly unrealistic. He sent to Franklin some samples of verse – postage due – to solicit his opinion. Franklin sometimes enjoyed writing poetry but knew it was no way to make a living.

Upon leaving the Golden Fan, Ralph promised Franklin the money he owed. Upon leaving for Berkshire, he promised to send money to Mrs T. Ralph's promises were as empty as his purse. Mrs T remained destitute. Franklin visited her several times and aided her financially. One time he 'attempted familiarities': big mistake. After parrying his advances, she told Ralph what had happened.

Franklin's lapse in judgement allowed Ralph a convenient indignation, providing a perfect excuse to avoid repaying him.[17]

Free from Ralph's influence, Franklin had a better chance to make his London dreams come true. His letter to Sloane shows that he had come prepared to meet the city's leading scientists. He brought American curiosities in lieu of calling cards. The letter may have been unconventional, but it peaked Sloane's interest. His vast collection at Bloomsbury Place – the nucleus of the British Museum – contained nothing like Franklin's asbestos purse. Sloane asked to see it and invited Franklin to his home to view his cabinet of curiosities.

Though Franklin never met Isaac Newton, England's most renowned early eighteenth-century scientist, Sloane was its second most renowned scientist. Whereas Newton championed scientific experimentation, Sloane's collecting activities represented an alternative, but no less valid approach to science. Britain's scientific community greatly respected Sloane, who understood the value of collecting as a means of broadening the knowledge of the world. He formed the centre of a network of gentlemen collectors throughout the British Empire.[18]

Keeping a cabinet had been an established custom in learned circles since the Renaissance. No matter how huge the cabinet, the personal collection of curiosities typically outgrew its confines and spilled over into the collector's living quarters. Once the original cabinet proved inadequate to hold all the objects their owner had assembled, the phrase became figurative. The collection was still called a 'cabinet of curiosities' no matter how far it exceeded the physical space designed to contain it.

Ideally intended to contribute to scientific knowledge, a collection of curiosities often performed personal and social functions. Some people displayed their curiosities to show off their intellect, taste and wealth. While the personal nature of a collection could detract from its scientific and historical value, cabinets of curiosities may be more important for what they say about their owners. A collection externalized the self, outwardly reflecting a person's mind.

Inside Sloane's handsome mansion at 3 Bloomsbury Place, Franklin viewed the doctor's massive collection. He left no description of what he saw, but other visitors can help reconstruct the experience. German bibliophile Zacharias Conrad von Uffenbach mentioned Sloane's politeness. Sloane escorted Uffenbach into a moderately sized room, the lower part of which was furnished with curiosity-filled cabinets. Shelves installed above the cabinets were lined with books. Erasmus Philipps noted that Sloane divided his natural curiosities into animal, mineral and vegetable. French surgeon Sauveur François Morand counted eleven rooms filled with curiosities.[19]

Visitors usually mentioned what curiosities impressed them most. Sloane showed Uffenbach a bird's nest from the West Indies, where they ate the nests as delicacies. Uffenbach wrote, 'Judging from its taste, appearance and feeling, I took it for a gum resin.'[20] Its taste? Sloane apparently broke off a little piece of bird's nest and fed it to his guest.

Philipps noted several stuffed and mounted animal specimens, including a Swedish owl. The most ghastly specimen he saw was a stillborn foetus. Sloane had a story to accompany this curiosity. Before her miscarriage, the woman did not know she was pregnant: she thought she had dropsy! She survived and subsequently gave birth to several healthy children. Sloane's story reveals the dynamic nature of his collection. He followed up the curiosities he collected. In this instance he learned what had happened years after the miscarriage. While visiting Sloane, Franklin could see how anecdotes enhanced a cabinet of curiosities.

The German physician Christian Erndl saw a coral-covered glass bottle. He described how it looked ('almost grown over with white coral'), who found it ('a curious mariner') and where he had found it ('on the shore in the Mediterranean'). Erndl conveyed his intellectual pleasure but ended the description slightly disappointed. If only the bottle were more exotic, the object would be more curious and thus more pleasurable.[21]

Sloane had man-made objects in his collection that had been obtained from around the world, including a pair of women's shoes from China. Swedish naturalist Pehr Kalm described them as 'the shoes of a grown up Chinese woman which were no bigger than those of a child of 2 or 3 years in Sweden'.[22] Kalm does not say why the Chinese shoes were so small. Chinese women did not have small feet naturally. Their tiny feet resulted from the cruel practice of foot binding. Since the Chinese saw small feet as signs of female pulchritude, girls' feet were often bound from early childhood to prevent them from growing properly.

An anecdote Franklin would adapt from John Selden's *Table-Talk* suggests that he also saw the cruel shoes in Sloane's collection. As Selden tells the story, the shoe in question is one Moses supposedly owned.[23] In Franklin's version, it becomes a Chinese shoe. Years later, Franklin told the story to Mary 'Polly' Stevenson, a bright, scientifically inclined young woman whom he mentored. His anecdote features a confident and perceptive female character:

> This prudence of not attempting to give reasons before one is sure of facts, I learnt from one of your sex, who, as Selden tells us, being in company with some gentlemen that were viewing and considering something which they call'd a Chinese shoe, and disputing earnestly about the manner of wearing it, and how it could possibly be put on; put in her word, and said modestly, 'Gentlemen, are you sure it is a shoe? Should not that be settled first?'[24]

Franklin had previously defended women against negative stereotypes. This anecdote similarly reflects his proto-feminist stance. Taking a curiosity that symbolizes the oppression of Chinese women, Franklin turned it into an anecdote illustrating both the importance of getting the facts straight and the power of the female intellect.

Sloane also showed off his 30,000-volume library. Both Morand and Erndl were drawn to Sloane's medical library, the largest in Europe. Sloane's collection of medical books must have impressed Franklin, whose knowledge of medicine would progress with the eighteenth century. Franklin would assemble the finest private medical library in Revolutionary America.[25]

A visit to Sloane's home could be fairly long. Kalm spent two hours viewing his collection. Philipps stayed for dinner. At the end of his four-hour visit, Uffenbach mentioned a new species of centipede and presented a specimen to Sloane. The story of Uffenbach's centipede parallels the story of Franklin's asbestos purse. Though Sloane paid for the purse, he appreciated the unusual item, which enhanced the quality of Franklin's visit to Bloomsbury Place.[26]

When Kalm and Franklin met in 1748, they discussed Sloane's curiosities. Besides telling Kalm about the asbestos purse, Franklin retold a pertinent anecdote from his personal repertoire. One time he sent a journeyman to the local paper mill to get some asbestos made into a sheet of paper. When the journeyman returned, Franklin rolled up the sheet and tossed it in the fire, but it did not burn. After the young man's amazement subsided, Franklin explained the properties of asbestos. The journeyman hoped to astound some friends with this curiosity. Unbeknownst to him, they understood the properties of asbestos. They played along, refusing to believe in fireproof paper. While the journeyman stirred the fire, they smeared the paper with fat. He threw the sheet in the fire, and it burst into flames. He was struck dumb. The others broke into laughter and revealed their trick.[27]

Recording his visit to Sloane, Kalm listed numerous items from Sloane's massive collection. When he saw Franklin's comparatively modest cabinet, Kalm had a much different experience and thus wrote a much different account. Franklin displayed a stone from New England. Kalm, who had studied under Carl Linnaeus in Uppsala, identified it as a mixture of asbestos and soapstone, *Lapis ollaris*. But Franklin did not just show Kalm the stone; he gave it to him. In other words, Franklin reversed the dynamics of collecting at his Philadelphia home. Whereas Sloane's visitors presented curiosities as a tribute to him, Franklin gave away objects of curiosity to show his hospitality and encourage further study.

Curiosities also performed a social function for Franklin. The stone he gave to Kalm is what triggered his humorous anecdote about the journeyman and the asbestos paper. Franklin understood that curiosities could spark discussion and debate, which they would keep doing throughout his life. He typically selected curiosities for his cabinet that would serve as conversation pieces.

Partway through his London sojourn, Franklin left Palmer's printing house for John Watts's. Located in Wild Court near Lincoln's Inn Fields, Watts's printing house was twice the size of Palmer's. Watts produced some of the early eighteenth century's handsomest books. Franklin eventually left the Golden Fan and moved closer to Wild Court, finding rooms at an Italian warehouse on Duke Street across from the Sardinian Chapel. This, the oldest Roman Catholic chapel in London, had been built in 1648 as an attachment to the residence of the Sardinian ambassador.

The Sardinian Chapel was fairly quiet when Franklin lived in the neighbourhood, but two decades earlier, it was the site of the first mission to another church by a member of the French Prophets, an eccentric Protestant sect Franklin knew about from a former member, Samuel Keimer. When he left the sect, Keimer wrote a tell-all book. Describing the physical movements during a prophesy, Keimer called them 'violent and strange agitations or shakings of body, loud and terrifying hiccups, and throbs, with many odd and

very surprizing postures'. Keimer enjoyed acting out the French
Prophets' enthusiastic agitations for his employees.[28]

The French Prophet who visited the Sardinian Chapel stripped
off all her clothes and ran up the aisle naked as Eve. She stopped
at the altar, 'where she appeared in several strange and indecent
postures, and being seemingly full of the pretended Spirit'.
Attempting to reform the Catholic parishioners, she prevailed for
fifteen minutes, that is, until the Holy Spirit left her, whereupon she
dressed and quietly walked away.[29]

Like many in the neighbourhood, Franklin's landlady was a
Roman Catholic. Though raised a Protestant, she had converted
to Catholicism upon her marriage to an Italian. Now a widow,
she retained fond memories of her husband, who had known
many distinguished Londoners stretching back to Charles II. She
peppered her conversation with anecdotes about famous people,
a thousand anecdotes Franklin said in a moment of hyperbole.
Regardless how many, her anecdotes reinforced the social and
historical value of personal stories.

Franklin often enjoyed supper with his landlady. His
autobiography describes what they ate: half an anchovy each
on a slice of bread with butter, washed down with half a pint
of ale. Then as now, great food is easy to find in an Italian
neighbourhood. It is not hard to imagine Franklin changing up his
anchovies and ale for some Bologna sausage and a nice Chianti.[30]

Outside Watts's shop, Franklin socialized with his co-worker
John Wigate. In May or June 1726 some of Wigate's friends from the
country visited. They wanted to sail up the Thames to Chelsea, and
Wigate asked Franklin to join them. They visited Chelsea Hospital,
where war veterans could spend the evening of their lives in peaceful
retirement. A long building with a central block and two wings of red
brick, Chelsea Hospital was designed by Christopher Wren. Followed
by Herman Melville and Orson Welles, Franklin was the first in a
series of notable Americans to visit the Chelsea pensioners.[31]

Wigate also brought his friends to Don Saltero's Coffee House in Cheyne Walk, possibly the highlight of the trip for Franklin. Don Saltero's was best known for its collection of curiosities, which attracted visitors from across London. Neither as wide-ranging as Sloane's collection, nor as systematic, Don Saltero's cabinet of curiosities was more democratic. Anyone who could afford a cup of coffee was welcome.

Though no coffee-house in London had as great a collection of curiosities as Don Saltero's, many contained some pertinent yet provocative objects. The Virginia Coffee House kept a live timber rattlesnake – *Crotalus horridus* – as a pet: an indication that Londoners already recognized the rattlesnake as an American icon. To compete with Don Saltero's, bun baker Richard Hand kept some display cases filled with curiosities at his nearby establishment, the

The Royal Hospital, Chelsea, as seen in 'Chelsea Pensioners', the fifth episode of *Around the World with Orson Welles* (1955). Welles hosted and directed all six episodes of this British television series.

Chelsea Bun House. In his autobiography, Franklin does not say whether he enjoyed Dick Hand's buns.

James Salter, the proprietor of Don Saltero's, changed his name to give it some Spanish flavour. He had learned from the best, having accompanied Sloane on a collecting trip to Jamaica. Salter took pride in his collection and enjoyed showing it to customers. He prominently displayed many curiosities in the front room. Larger items – stuffed and mounted animals, skeletons, primitive weaponry – covered the walls and ceiling.

Salter regularly published catalogues of his curiosities. None survive from the time of Franklin's visit, but one published a few years later indicates what he could have seen. Eighteenth-century collectors typically divided their curiosities into two general categories: natural and man-made. Salter's can be divided similarly. He also had several items of Americana, including a stuffed armadillo, some stuffed hummingbirds, a buffalo skin, a large Indian club and some tomahawks.

The numerical order of the catalogued items may reflect their physical organization inside Don Saltero's. Several ancient Chinese objects appear together, so do some decorative snuff-boxes. Two related items pair a natural curiosity with a man-made one: 'a large worm that eats into the keel of ships in the West Indies' and 'a piece of a worm-eaten keel'.[32]

These clusters seem designed to make patrons think. The various Chinese objects – different items from one place – encourage visitors to consider what they have in common, how they collectively reflect Chinese culture. The snuff-boxes – similar items from different places – encourage people to discern how they differ. The worm-and-keel cluster asks a question. More and more British ships were travelling to far-flung parts of the globe, but they faced a problem: a wormlike mollusc that threatened trade and exploration. How could these termites of the sea be stopped?

The visit to the curiosity-filled coffee-house left Franklin in an ecstatic mood. As he and the others boarded their boat, Wigate boasted about Franklin's natatory prowess. Their curiosity piqued, they asked Franklin about it. He answered by stripping off his clothes and jumping into the river. As they sailed back, he swam alongside the boat all the way to Blackfriars demonstrating his versatility as a swimmer.

His swimming ability was not solely a matter of athleticism. After he had learned to swim as a child, he studied the subject, reading Melchisédec Thévenot's *Art of Swimming* and practising its directions. To crawl, to dog paddle, to tread water, to do the back stroke and the breast stroke: Thévenot described these and many other movements. Franklin's fitness and flexibility let him perform all sorts of underwater acrobatics. He amazed Wigate's friends. Never before had they encountered swimming strokes like his.

It is crucial to understand that this experience occurred directly after the visit to Don Saltero's. Franklin came away from the coffee-house longing to establish his own cabinet of curiosities. Though he could not begin forming one yet, he recognized an alternative. In the devotional literature of the previous century, the human body had often been figured as a cabinet. John Bunyan, whose writings Franklin had known since childhood, compares the two in *The Greatness of the Soul*. As a cabinet is made to hold 'things that are choice', the body is made to hold the soul.[33]

Franklin borrowed this figurative comparison, stripped it of its religious meaning and literalized it. Swimming for an audience, he transformed his body into a fleshy cabinet of curiosities. The words that describe this episode in his autobiography – exhibit, novelty, pleasure, surprise – are much the same words contemporaries used to describe viewing a cabinet of curiosities.

Whereas Sloane stressed the bond between curiosities and anecdotes, this swimming experience let Franklin know that curiosities need not be material objects. The body could be turned into an impromptu cabinet with the possibility of displaying many curious athletic moves. The mind, too, could hold curiosities of its own. Not only adjuncts to the cabinet, anecdotes could be curiosities in and of themselves: verbal curiosities.

Anecdotes have a major advantage over physical curiosities. Unlike objects in a cabinet, anecdotes are portable. The penchant for personal anecdotes Franklin would cultivate for the rest of his life emerged in London from the combined influence of Sloane's curiosities, Don Saltero's coffee-house, the thousand anecdotes of Franklin's Duke Street landlady and his swimming exhibit in the Thames. Franklin's anecdotes were curiosities he could display whenever he wished. He did not need to take anyone to his home to display his curiosities. Franklin stored his best curiosities in his memory, and he could access and display them in conversation.

2

The Power of the Printed Word

After eighteen months in London, Franklin found himself at a crossroads. Wigate proposed a poor-man's Grand Tour. They could travel around Europe together, pausing to work as printers whenever they needed cash. The idea was tempting, but responsibility tugged from a different direction. Denham, who thought Franklin should return to Philadelphia, offered him a job. A mercantile career, Denham argued, would not preclude occasional travel. Franklin accepted.

On 21 July 1726 Franklin and Denham set sail aboard the *Berkshire*. Two months later, they remained at sea, but Franklin felt they were getting close to home. He ended his journal entry for 24 September with a heroic couplet: 'On either side the parted billows flow/ While the black ocean foams and roars below.' Derived from Alexander Pope's then-recent translation of Homer's *Odyssey*, these lines occur shortly before Ulysses spots Ithaca. With this couplet, Franklin compares himself to Ulysses: he, too, was returning home from a long and life-shaping adventure.[1]

The *Berkshire* entered a meadow of sargasso four days later. Franklin dropped a boat hook and fished out a tangle. He noted the shape of its leaves and measured their length. What caught his attention most were some tiny, heart-shaped shellfish on its stalks. The smaller ones resembled oysters; the larger were animated, opening their shells and extending crablike claws.

Watching a little crab crawl around, Franklin hypothesized that the other creatures were crab embryos. To test his hypothesis, he put some shellfish-infested sargasso in a glass jar with salt water to see if more crabs developed. One formed; the rest died. The survivor was sufficient: it proved the smaller ones were crab embryos. What Franklin found was *Cancer minutus*. He did not discover this species. Christopher Columbus had found it in 1492.

The next night Franklin shifted his attention from sea to sky. The subject of astronomy, a lifelong interest, often shows up in his writings. In *Poor Richard's Almanack,* for example, he contrasts Copernicus's view of the solar system with Ptolemy's. Franklin's folksy comparison demonstrates the absurdity of Ptolemaic geocentrism. Ptolemy resembled 'a whimsical cook, who, instead of turning his meat in roasting, should fix that, and contrive to have his whole fire, kitchen and all, whirling continually round it'.[2]

Having brought a current almanac from London, Franklin knew a lunar eclipse would occur Thursday night, 29 September. Franklin's extensive almanac collection at the American Philosophical Society contains none from 1726 but does show that Salem Pearse's *Coelestial Diary* was a personal favourite. Pearse said the eclipse would begin in London at 3.52 a.m. and last for two hours. Unsure when it would begin at sea – remember there was still no accurate way to determine longitude – Franklin would stay up and take observations.

Pearse said the eclipse foretold 'wars, quarrels, duels, massacres, etc: hot air, thunder and lightning, and shipwrecks, and loss by pyrates at sea'.[3] Franklin's interpretation is more pragmatic. By carefully observing the eclipse, he determined the position of the *Berkshire* and computed the remaining distance. Fellow passengers welcomed his results. According to Franklin, they were only a hundred leagues from Philadelphia.

His behaviour aboard the *Berkshire* established a pattern Franklin would repeat on subsequent ocean crossings. He could always find something to stoke his curiosity. His Atlantic explorations prompted the Underwater Society of America to adopt Franklin as its godfather two centuries later. Jacques Cousteau's editor called Franklin the first American oceanographer. Cousteau appreciated the swim fins that Franklin invented as a boy, which anticipated ones he would use on his undersea adventures.[4]

Proving a traditional sailor saying that Melville would record for posterity – 'There are no Sundays off soundings' – the *Berkshire* crew took soundings on Sunday 9 October. They struck ground at 25 fathoms (45 m). A member of Franklin's mess went aloft and cried out, 'Land! Land!' Franklin captured the moment: 'In less than an hour we could descry it from the deck, appearing like tufts of trees. I could not discern it so soon as the rest; my eyes were dimmed with the suffusion of two small drops of joy.'[5]

On Monday morning the pilot boat approached, bringing the *Berkshire* a peck of apples, the most delicious Franklin had ever tasted. He felt sure that they would reach Philadelphia by nightfall on Tuesday, but the *Berkshire* cast anchor 6 miles (10 km) out. Happily, some young men sailing for pleasure offered him a ride into town. About ten o'clock Tuesday night, 11 October, Franklin landed at Philadelphia.

His new job began the next day. Franklin and Denham had to unload the retail goods Denham had shipped aboard the *Berkshire* and find a storefront to rent. They found a suitable house on Water (now, Front) Street, two doors from the Crooked Billet. They could sleep upstairs and operate the store downstairs, which had plenty of shelving and a built-in counter.[6]

Denham stocked bolts of fabric: calico, a brightly coloured cotton cloth as strong as silk; osnaburg, a hard-wearing linen useful for work clothes; and shalloon, a closely woven woollen fabric used for linings. They also sold ready-made articles of clothing: caps, gloves, socks. In addition, they stocked household goods – soap, candles, lanterns, kettles – and workmen's tools: coopers' axes, carpenters' axes and scythes. Denham stocked a few grocery items, including coffee and garlic.[7] This last item may reflect a taste Franklin developed while in his Italian neighbourhood in London.

Franklin kept the books and manned the store. A great talker, he naturally became a good salesman. Having worked in his father's tallow chandlery, he knew all about soap and candles. The rest he learned as he went. Franklin occasionally acquired items he needed. With the onset of autumn, he bought himself a new cap, but it could not guard against pleurisy, the pulmonary affliction that brought down King Charlemagne. Pleurisy struck Franklin late that winter.

Unaware of infection – its typical cause – contemporary physicians attributed pleurisy, like everything, to an imbalance of humours. Treatment involved bloodletting and induced vomiting: let 10 ounces of blood per day for three or four days in a row, and take ipecac the third day.[8] Franklin's pleurisy prevented him from working. Denham, who hired a replacement for Franklin in March 1727, fell ill himself that year. Franklin recovered; Denham did not. The nature of Denham's illness is unknown, but it lingered into the next year, when he succumbed to it.

Once Franklin had recovered, he unsuccessfully sought retail work elsewhere. Keimer, now operating both a stationer's shop and a printing house, asked him to return. Wanting to concentrate on his retail business, he hoped his former employee would manage his printing house. With no other prospects, Franklin accepted his old boss's lucrative offer.

Franklin oversaw a staff of five, including Hugh Meredith, whose love of drink sometimes superseded his passion for reading; Stephen Potts, a great wit but a little lazy; and George Webb, an Oxford scholar turned indentured servant. Keimer had hired Meredith to operate the press and Potts to work as a bookbinder; neither possessed the requisite skills. Keimer wanted Franklin to train his employees. Once they acquired the necessary skills, he would be superfluous, so Keimer could fire him.

Aware Keimer was taking advantage, Franklin nonetheless enjoyed the work and the others: 'I began to live very agreeably; for they all respected me, the more as they found Keimer incapable of instructing them, and that from me they learnt something daily.' Franklin was learning much himself: 'I also engrav'd several things on occasion. I made the ink, I was warehouse-man and every thing.'[9]

Hearing a loud noise one early October day, Franklin poked his head out the window to see what was the matter. 'Mind your own business,' Keimer, then outside, yelled to Franklin. Neighbours witnessed his abusive treatment. Upon returning, he gave Franklin three months to clear out. Franklin did not need three minutes. He left immediately.

That evening Franklin and Meredith discussed what to do. If Franklin had his own printing house, Meredith argued, he could drive Keimer out of business. Franklin liked the idea, but lacked the capital. Meredith proposed a partnership. His father would advance the necessary funds. Franklin soon ordered the equipment they needed. Months would pass before everything arrived from London, so Franklin returned to work for Keimer on his request, without understanding his sudden change of heart.

Franklin socialized with Meredith, Potts and Webb outside the office. In autumn 1727 they formed the Junto, a club for personal and social improvement. They limited its membership to twelve; other Philadelphia men quickly filled the remaining slots. All shared a love of books. Botanist, poet and wit Joseph Breintnall became Franklin's best friend in the Junto.

Other charter members included the cool-headed, warm-hearted William Coleman; Robert Grace, an entrepreneur, generous and gregarious; and Nicholas Scull, a part-time surveyor who operated the Indian Head Tavern, where the Junto first gathered. Scull left the only contemporary account of a Junto meeting, which he wrote in verse.[10]

As some members left the Junto, new ones took their places, including Samuel Rhoads, a carpenter who would develop into a leading architect, and Thomas Hopkinson, a lawyer and merchant who had emigrated from England in 1731. Hopkinson added much to their Friday night gatherings. His obituarist would characterize his social behaviour: 'In the hours of recreation, he had the particular faculty of tempering the facetious with the grave, in so agreeable a manner, as made his conversation both delightful and instructive.'[11]

The Junto met every Friday night. Scull's poem says they initially discussed some scientific queries, thus affirming the Junto's rules, which required each member, in turn, to prepare for discussion at least one query about morality, politics or natural philosophy. Franklin typically tested out his ideas in the Junto before publishing them. *A Modest Enquiry into the Nature and Necessity of a Paper Currency*, his first political tract, presumably took shape in the Junto. Franklin successfully argued that additional paper currency would improve business conditions and enhance the Pennsylvania economy.

Several community projects began similarly. After proposing a fire insurance plan to the Junto, Franklin would create the first fire insurance company in America. In addition, he organized the Union Fire Company, Philadelphia's first. Junto members also discussed police reform. An eighteenth-century Serpico, Franklin exposed graft and corruption among Philadelphia's nightwatchmen. While advocating police reform, he understood it could be tedious and time-consuming. Years would pass before the city adopted the reforms he proposed.

The Junto's rules required each member to read aloud an original essay once every three months. In Scull's poem, an unnamed member demonstrates a 'strength of thought in lofty language'. The queries and the essay together formed the Junto's main business. Members next turned to music, poetry and drink.

Scull continues,

> Business being ore a difrent scene appeard
> First the soft flute in pleasing notes is heard
> Next see the juice the witty bards inspire
> With bright ideas and poetick fire.[12]

The music varied from one Friday to the next, depending upon who was playing what. Franklin's ability to play the violin and the guitar are well known. Lemay is confident he could play the oboe, as well.[13] Scull does not say what they drank, but his account books provide a clue. In 1728 the Junto began meeting at Scull's new establishment, the Bear Tavern. One night Franklin and Meredith each spent five pence: the cost of a quart of 'best beer'.[14] Reading poetry, playing music, drinking beer: life does not get much better.

Franklin soon discovered why Keimer wanted him back. The New Jersey Assembly had asked if Keimer could print currency that would be difficult to counterfeit. Given this lucrative opportunity, he said he could do it. Keimer could not but knew that Franklin could. That's why he reconciled with Franklin. In February 1728 they went to Burlington, New Jersey, where Franklin created the first copper-plate press in America and designed and cut several hard-to-counterfeit ornaments for the bills. Since the New Jersey legislators closely oversaw their work, Franklin befriended many influential men and, therefore, made many important business contacts.

In mid-May, shortly after he and Keimer returned from New Jersey, Franklin and Meredith quit. They left amicably; Keimer was unaware the two would become his competitors. Their new equipment had arrived from London, and they found a suitable house on Market Street, a busy commercial street, which Breintnall captured in verse. His poem welcomes readers to enjoy Philadelphia's growing prosperity: 'Step, gently rising, o'er the pebbly way,/ And see the shops their tempting wares display.'[15] Franklin and Meredith set up their press, distributed the type into the upper and lower cases and opened the New Printing Office.

The office did much job printing: apprenticeship bonds, arbitration bonds, bills of lading, book labels, legal forms, lottery tickets, marriage surety bonds, mortgage bonds, powers of attorney, quit-rent notices, real-estate advertisements, receipts and warrants. Franklin also printed currency for Pennsylvania, using an innovative system of nature printing to guard against counterfeiting. Franklin devised a way to print unique impressions of tree leaves as part of individual bills. Before starting his own almanac, he published those of others. For Philadelphia's churches, he printed catechisms, psalm books, religious tracts and sermons. Books he printed at his own risk included conduct manuals, medical handbooks, poems, songbooks and spelling books.

Free of his indenture, Webb approached Franklin and Meredith for a job. They had nothing for him, but since they were planning a newspaper, they might need him soon. Webb, who had written newspaper articles in his native Gloucester, liked the idea of editing a paper but knew Franklin would serve as editor, leaving him little but manual labour. Webb revealed Franklin's secret to Keimer, who quickly announced his own newspaper, which precluded Franklin and Meredith from starting theirs.

Keimer quashed whatever hopes Webb had for editing the paper. He would edit it himself, so Webb's duplicitous behaviour gained him nothing. The first number of *The Universal Instructor in All Arts and Sciences: and Pennsylvania Gazette* appeared on 24 December 1728. Keimer's title reflects his long-range plan for the paper, which would take advantage of the new-found interest in general knowledge that English encyclopaedist Ephraim Chambers represented.

After Chambers announced his encyclopaedia, he attracted some American subscribers, including Philadelphia polymath

Stanley Massey Arthurs, *Franklin the Printer*, *c*. 1914, lithograph after painting.

James Logan; James Montgomerie, governor of New York and New Jersey; and New York physician, historian and botanist Cadwallader Colden. Chambers's *Cyclopaedia* appeared in 1728, and copies reached Philadelphia that September. When Keimer started serializing it, he was reprinting a brand-new work. He never calculated how long the serialization would take. Franklin did. Without exaggeration, he reckoned it would take fifty years to finish.[16]

Reaching 'ABO' in his fifth issue, 21 January 1729, Keimer reprinted Chambers's article about abortion, a subject encompassing miscarriages. The article suggests that Keimer was reprinting Chambers without considering how Philadelphia readers might react. But Keimer, who was fascinated with the female body, revised and expanded Chambers's text. His revisions have previously gone unnoticed.

Keimer inserted a definition of 'placenta' in brackets, which proved pointless because he accidentally dropped the line of Chambers's text containing the word 'placenta'. After the insertion, Keimer continued Chambers's list of causes for miscarriage: 'excess of eating, long fasting or waking, the use of busks for the shape, offensive smells, violent purgatives; and, in the general, any thing that tends to promote the *menses*.' Keimer italicized 'menses' for emphasis; Chambers had not. Keimer inserted another bracketed passage to define 'tenesmus': 'a continu'd desire of going to stool'.[17]

Reading the abortion article, Franklin saw his advantage and attacked, writing two pseudonymous items for Bradford's *American Weekly Mercury*. 'Martha Careful' condemns Keimer for exposing female secrets and threatens to tug his beard and make him an example for his immodesty. 'Caelia Shortface' goes further, threatening to cut off his right ear. Caelia Shortface speaks like a Quaker, but her closing words reflect Franklin's opinion: 'If thou hath nothing else to put in thy *Gazette*, lay it down.'[18]

Franklin, who could be a shrewd and ruthless businessman, found another way to damage Keimer's *Gazette*. He would contribute a series of satirical essays to Bradford's *Mercury*, hoping to enhance its popularity and thus assure Keimer's failure. Aware the essays would increase his circulation, Bradford agreed, perhaps without realizing that once Franklin had run Keimer out of business, he might turn against him.

'The Busy-Body', which began on 4 February 1729, marks an advance in Franklin's writing. Whereas he had invented a back story for Silence Dogood, Franklin felt no need to create one for this new persona. Omitting personal detail, Mr Busy-Body lets his writing style reflect his personality, evincing a cosmopolitanism alien to Silence Dogood. To illustrate his arguments, Mr Busy-Body borrows examples from around the globe.

The fourth number draws on Near East culture to make its point. Delineating the Turkish manner of entertaining visitors, Mr Busy-Body quotes Henry Maundrell's *Journey from Aleppo to Jerusalem*. He claims to quote his source directly, but Franklin carefully revised Maundrell, removing extraneous detail. Mr Busy-Body concentrates on the subject of hospitality, quoting the parts about serving sherbet and perfuming the visitors' beards.[19]

In the first week of March, Franklin published 'Busy-Body, No. 5'. Joseph Breintnall joined in the fun and wrote the sixth and seventh numbers. Learning about Breintnall's contributions, Keimer responded in rhyme:

> But prithee tell me, art thou mad,
> To mix good writing with the bad?
> Fie, Sir, let all be of a piece,
> Spectators, swans, or Joseph's geese.[20]

Keimer's verse applies a proverb: everyone thinks their geese are swans. This proverb – a Franklin favourite – reminded contemporary moralist Oswald Dykes of the man who thought his farts smelled like frankincense.[21]

The serialization of Chambers's *Cyclopaedia* continued inexorably. The third week of July, Keimer published the first instalment of 'Air', which he would continue every week for the next two months. By 25 September Keimer was only two issues from completing the article, but he had had enough. He sold the *Universal Instructor* to Franklin and Meredith, closed his printing house and left town.

Keimer did not disappear into thin air. He would remain a force on the colonial publishing scene, relocating to Barbados, where he started its first newspaper, the *Barbados Gazette*, in 1731 and kept it going for years. Keimer edited selections from the paper as *Caribbeana*, a major anthology in the literary history of Barbados. Though Franklin would depict him as a bearded buffoon in his autobiography, he followed Keimer's career and obtained a copy of *Caribbeana*.[22]

Franklin and Meredith issued the first number of their newspaper without missing a beat – or a week. The 2 October issue was simply titled the *Pennsylvania Gazette*. Selling the paper to Franklin, Keimer had thrown in his copy of Chambers, but Franklin dropped the encyclopaedia project.[23] Philadelphia readers surfeited on air could breathe a sigh of relief. Franklin's front page editorial encouraged readers to contribute articles, which would broaden the newspaper's perspective and enhance its authenticity.

Franklin's first issue reveals the work and thought he put into it. Pennsylvania's annual election took place on 1 October that year. He reported the results the very next day! His report gives the election returns from Chester County as well as Philadelphia County. He must have stationed a man with a fast horse at the Chester County Courthouse that night to await the results. Franklin ended the article apologizing for the absence of returns from Bucks and Lancaster, two more distant counties. Though characteristic, this self-effacing apology detracts from Franklin's extraordinary achievement. His planning and expedience put him a week ahead of Bradford, who would not report the election until 9 October.

The finest articles in the *Pennsylvania Gazette* are those Franklin wrote himself. Consider 'A Witch Trial at Mount Holly'. (Titles facilitate the discussion of Franklin's newspaper articles, but most, like this one, have been assigned by modern editors.) 'Witch Trial' manifests Franklin's love of hoaxes. At Mount Holly, New Jersey, the story goes, some local men and women were accused of sorcery. They supposedly made their neighbours' sheep dance and their hogs sing. Franklin's vivid imagery is delightfully absurd, but some readers took the hoax seriously. It was reprinted as fact well into the nineteenth century.[24]

'Letter of the Drum' is a satirical tale recalling 'The Drummer of Tedworth', an English ghost story. Four reverend gentlemen travel from Philadelphia to a distant religious conference. At their lodging house, two preachers share one room, the other two share another. American writers often tell stories about the humorous situations that arise when travellers share rooms. 'The Spouter-Inn', the third chapter of *Moby-Dick*, is the greatest example of this motif in American literature; 'Letter of the Drum' is the first.

Attempting to sleep, two preachers hear strange noises as night falls. Suddenly one is seized by the big toe and almost dragged from the bed. Once the ghostly drum starts beating, his toe is mysteriously released. Franklin has the two preachers hoist their knees to their noses to prevent any further attacks, creating a hilarious portrait of fear. As the ominous drum gets louder and louder, the two feel 'a most prodigious weight on them, heavier . . . than the night-mare'.[25]

Sometimes words have two meanings. The word 'nightmare' had yet to gain the connotation of a frightening dream. In Franklin's day, it meant a feeling of suffocation during sleep; it was also a synonym for a succubus, a demon in female form that descends upon men in their sleep to enjoy carnal intercourse.

The succubus turns out to be a preacher from the other room who has snuck into theirs to scare them. Comparing a minister to a succubus, Franklin enhanced his satire with some bawdy, sacrilegious innuendo.

Franklin was a funny guy. The slightest little squibs he wrote to fill the spare blank spaces of the *Gazette* contain priceless nuggets of humour. After describing a thunderstorm that had done great damage in New York, he reported a story about lightning that hit closer to home. In Bucks County, lightning struck so near one young man that it melted the pewter button on the waistband of his breeches. Franklin quipped, ''Tis well nothing else thereabouts, was made of pewter.'[26]

In April 1730, before the New Printing Office had hardly got off the ground, it faced a financial crisis of existential proportions. The merchant who had imported the press and types had only received half his fee, so he sued Franklin and Meredith for the rest. Franklin feared they would lose their entire printing plant. The Junto came to the rescue: Coleman and Grace each offered to advance Franklin the necessary funds – with one caveat. Neither wanted him to continue with Meredith, who, they said, 'was often seen drunk in the streets, and playing at low games in alehouses'.[27]

Meredith's father had hoped that business responsibilities and Franklin's influence would cure his son's debauchery. They had not. Franklin dissolved their partnership and became sole owner of the New Printing Office. Meredith left for North Carolina and turned farmer. Within a decade, he was back in Philadelphia. Franklin advanced Meredith hundreds of chapbooks, so he could enter the chapman's trade. With a pack full of books, Meredith left Philadelphia and faded into the countryside. Franklin never saw him again.

The New Printing Office proved quite successful. The *Pennsylvania Gazette* became the most widely read paper in colonial America. Franklin also established several partnerships, starting in 1731, when he sponsored his journeyman Thomas Whitmarsh's printing house in Charleston, South Carolina. Franklin advanced him the necessary equipment and materials in exchange for a third of the profits. From 1736 Franklin also took an active role in the papermaking business, sponsoring American paper manufacture and wholesaling locally made paper.

In 1736 Franklin was selected clerk of the Pennsylvania Assembly. Though he would serve in that capacity for several years, he often found the legislative debates tedious and sought ways to amuse himself during the dull moments. Franklin used his mathematical skills to make magic squares, that is, big squares containing lots of little squares into each of which he would write a different number. Franklin created 8×8 squares and 16×16 squares. The challenge was to make every row and every column add up to the exact same total. Franklin sometimes went further, making the diagonals add up to the same total, as well.

His political appointments enhanced Franklin's commercial endeavours. As assembly clerk, he befriended many of the legislators, who threw much of the colony's official printing his way. In 1737 Franklin became postmaster of Philadelphia, a position that, while not lucrative in itself, further enhanced his business opportunities, letting him sell more newspapers and more newspaper advertising.[28]

Franklin issued his first *Poor Richard's Almanack* in late 1732, introducing his persona, the starry-eyed, henpecked Richard Saunders. Since almanacs gave colonial printers a steady annual income, competition could be fierce. To lure readers, Franklin sometimes used scatological humour. *Poor Richard's Almanack* typically begins with Saunders's epistle to his readers. The introductory epistle for 1739 ridicules astrology. Saunders explains how an astrologer uses the stars to predict the weather and, in so doing, depicts him as a voyeur-pervert:

He spies perhaps Virgo (or the Virgin); she turns her head round as it were to see if any body observ'd her; then crouching down gently, with her hands on her knees, she looks wistfully for a while right forward. He judges rightly what she's about: And having calculated the distance and allow'd time for its falling, finds that next spring we shall have a fine April shower.[29]

This same almanac reveals that Franklin had been reading Rabelais lately. His 'True Prognostication, for 1739' is a revision of Rabelais's 'Most Certain, True and Infallible Pantagruelian Prognostication', which ends *Gargantua and Pantagruel*. Franklin knew what he could get away with – and what he couldn't. Condensing Rabelais, he removed the following prediction: 'Many a ones yard will hang down and dangle, for want of leathern pouches.' Franklin also omitted Rabelais's prediction that people afflicted with the 'wild-squirt will often prostitute their blind cheeks to the bog-house'.[30]

Franklin did not use raunchy jokes gratuitously. His scatological humour was not a matter of farts for farts' sake. Most of his Poor Richardisms are not original in terms of concept, but they are original in terms of diction and syntax. One traditional saying goes like this: 'Who is in fault suspects everybody.' In *Henry VI, Part 3*, Shakespeare eloquently rewords the traditional saying to make it memorable: 'Suspicion always haunts the guilty mind.' Franklin makes the saying memorable by interjecting some scatological humour: 'He that is conscious of a stink in his breeches, is jealous of every wrinkle in another's nose.'[31]

Directly or indirectly, Rabelais would resurface in Franklin's subsequent writings. 'Old Mistresses Apologue', written a half dozen years later, takes the form of a letter to an unmarried friend considering a love affair. It resembles Pantagruel's advice to Panurge, when Panurge is considering marriage. The first part of 'Old Mistresses Apologue' recommends marriage; the second offers advice about taking a lover. The second part is facetious, but its deadpan manner gives it a mock seriousness that enhances the humour.

Franklin tells his friend to look towards older women to find a lover. They have several advantages over younger ones, not least of which is their vast experience. Older women have no drawbacks. Their decrepit physical appearance is not a disadvantage. Since the body ages more slowly than the face, all the friend needs to do before making love to an old woman is put a basket over her head. Franklin exclaims the final advantage in favour of old women: 'They are so grateful!!'[32]

Between the time he returned from London in 1726 and the decade's end, Franklin's own marriage prospects faced much uncertainty. Deborah regretted having forsaken him to marry John Rogers, a lout and a cad and a deadbeat. Rogers deserted Deborah, fleeing Philadelphia for the West Indies in December 1727. One rumour said he had a wife abroad. Another said he perished at sea. There was a third possibility: Rogers could return at any moment. Benjamin remained fond of Deborah, but, given her situation, he hesitated to reignite their romance and looked elsewhere for affection.

The image of Franklin as a wise and witty old sage has become so deeply ingrained in American culture that it is sometimes difficult to picture him as a healthy young man with a healthy young man's desires. What did Franklin know about sex and how did he know it? That he invented a ruse about getting a girl pregnant when he was seventeen suggests a fair amount of knowledge.

Keimer, oddly enough, had much to say about sex. The very subject would set his beard a-wagging. His experience with the French Prophets had given him racy stories to tell his journeymen. While under divinely inspired agitations, a prophet named John Glover 'imitated conjugal affection with a prophetess on a bed, before a number of believers'. Like the French Prophets' other physical agitations, Glover's behaviour was considered a sign. A sign of what Keimer could not tell, unless it was a sign that 'the prophet would willingly perform that in reality, which he did there shew but in effigies'.[33]

Briefly mentioning his own sexual escapades in his autobiography, Franklin revealed that his desire was strong enough that not even the risk of venereal disease could deter him:

> That hard-to-be-govern'd passion of youth had hurried
> me frequently into intrigues with low women that fell
> in my way, which were attended with some expence
> and great inconvenience, besides a continual risque
> to my health by a distemper which of all things I
> dreaded, tho' by great good luck I escaped it.[34]

Precisely where young Franklin's sexual liaisons took place remains a mystery. While serving on the grand jury some years later, he mentioned a Philadelphia neighbourhood known as 'Hell Town'. Located on Third Street just south of Race Street, Hell Town consisted of a long row of single-storey 'disorderly houses'. Franklin may have escaped venereal disease, but the dubious salubrity of Hell Town's brothels suggests that *Cancer minutus* was not the only little crab he encountered as a young man. *Pthirus pubis* may have paid him a visit. Happily, the New Printing Office stocked an 'ointment for the itch' that would kill 'all sorts of lice'.[35]

To control his sexual desire, Franklin added chastity to his list of thirteen moral virtues: 'Rarely use venery but for health or offspring. Never to dulness, weakness, or the injury of your own or another's reputation.' Revising this admonition for his autobiography, Franklin turned the last word into a conjoined pair: 'peace or reputation'.[36] The revision aligns Franklin's autobiography with contemporary fiction. Many eighteenth-century seduction novels use the same word pair. Virtuous heroines must constantly guard their 'peace and reputation' against lascivious pursuers.

Franklin's sexual indiscretion resulted in an unplanned pregnancy. Around 1728 one of his lovers gave birth to a baby boy, whom Franklin named William and agreed to raise. The identity of William's mother has escaped history. The autobiography's 'low women' have prompted conjectures that she was a kitchen maid, an oyster wench or maybe a street-corner strumpet. She was probably not a prostitute. If she were, Franklin could not have been sure he was the father. She must have been a woman of higher status, one unwilling to raise or even acknowledge the boy.[37]

Picturing Franklin raising William at the New Printing Office recalls how Charlie Chaplin's tramp raises his foundling in *The Kid*. Rearing a son while running a business no doubt created moments of hilarity, but there was nothing funny about Franklin's marital situation. An illegitimate child severely limited his prospects. After William's birth, Benjamin and Deborah rekindled their romance. She hesitated to assume the burden of a stepson, but, given her situation, she had few marriage prospects. Deborah, bless her heart, agreed to raise William as her own. Because Rogers's fate remained unknown, Benjamin and Deborah could not legally wed. They formed a common-law marriage, announcing to friends on 1 September 1730 that they would henceforth live together as man and wife.[38]

Franklin's family life did not stifle his social and intellectual life. He still attended Junto meetings on Friday nights. At one, he proposed that members club together their personal book collections to form a library, which would far exceed what any could assemble individually. Though the Junto accepted the proposal, the plan for a communal library did not work. In this instance, Franklin failed to recognize the personal importance of books. Not merely repositories of ideas, they embody the personality of their owners, who dislike letting them out of their sight.

The failure of the communal library had a major impact on American library history: in 1731 it led Franklin and his friends to form the Library Company of Philadelphia. Each subscriber bought a share, providing the capital to purchase its core collection. Annual dues would help maintain and grow the collection. By the second week of November, Franklin had generated enough interest in the library to start receiving subscriptions. Potential members gathered at the Bear Tavern to subscribe. Grace was first in line, Hopkinson second, Franklin third and Breintnall, having agreed to serve as secretary, fifth. Within a year, they received their first shipment of books. The model for subscription libraries throughout colonial America, the Library Company became the intellectual centre of Philadelphia. It thrives today. Though its purpose has changed – it is now a major research library – the Library Company remains the intellectual centre of Philadelphia.

Few contributed to the development of the Library Company more than London mercer Peter Collinson, whose lucrative business involved importing and exporting fine fabrics but whose passion was botany. Needing someone to procure books for its holdings, Breintnall contacted Collinson, who volunteered to serve as its London agent. He would continue in that capacity for many years, helping to choose, purchase and ship books to Philadelphia, but refusing to accept any remuneration.[39]

When some local men started the St John's Lodge of Freemasons in 1730 – the first Masonic lodge in America – Franklin was disappointed they had not invited him. He finagled his way into the organization by publishing a satirical essay about freemasonry in the *Gazette*. His satire essentially told the masons it would be better to have a witty newspaper editor with them than against them. They got the message. In January 1731, the month after the article appeared, the St John's Lodge voted to admit Franklin.

From his first lodge meeting in February, Franklin attended the regular meetings on the first Monday of each month and the annual

June meetings each St John's Day. He became a great favourite. He wrote a drinking song – 'Fair Venus Calls' – and enjoyed singing it at lodge meetings. The first verse praises the pleasures of love, but the chorus disagrees:

> O No!
> Not so!
> For honest souls know,
> Friends and a bottle still bear the bell.[40]

Franklin's work complemented his Masonic activities. In May 1734 he reprinted James Anderson's *Constitutions of the Free Masons*, the standard Masonic handbook. The timing of this publication – the month before the annual elections – reflects Franklin's opportunism and the power of the printed word. Sure enough, his lodge brothers elected him grand master on St John's Day. A gala attended by the governor and other prominent figures that evening marked Franklin's public recognition as a community leader.[41]

Once he joined the St John's Lodge, Franklin published a favourable article about freemasonry in the *Gazette*. Since members were sworn to secrecy, he could not write anything himself, but he found something suitable in Chambers's *Cyclopaedia*. The article calls freemasonry 'truly good and laudable, as it tends to promote friendship, society, mutual assistance, and good-fellowship'.[42]

Though Franklin had abandoned Keimer's plan to serialize Chambers, he saw value in articles coinciding with current events or personal aims. Some of Chambers's articles could entertain the curious and help those who lacked good libraries. Upon announcing that he would abandon the serialization, he promised to reprint additional items from Chambers when pertinent.[43]

In his third issue of the *Gazette*, Franklin reprinted Chambers's article about hemp to encourage its cultivation in colonial America for the production of naval stores. The article gives its scientific name: *Cannabis*. (The Linnaean taxonomy, which would establish the binomial genus-plus-species nomenclature, remained a decade away.) The article also says how to grow hemp and describes its properties and uses. It even explains hemp's physiological effects when inhaled or ingested. Its strong smell 'affects the head', and its pollen, when dissolved in liquor, 'is said to turn them who drink thereof, stupid'.[44]

When news of a smallpox epidemic in New England reached Philadelphia in May 1730, Franklin reprinted the article on inoculation from Chambers, which describes the clinical procedure and advocates its validity for guarding against smallpox. Franklin became one of Philadelphia's leading advocates for inoculation – even in the face of personal tragedy. On 21 November 1736 Francis Franklin, the first child Benjamin and Deborah had together, died of smallpox. He was only four.

Rumours circulated that Francis had died from inoculation, which Franklin promptly quashed. He told readers his son had contracted smallpox through infection, not inoculation. He had been planning to inoculate little Franky once he recovered from another illness. Less than a year after his death, Thomas Hopkinson's wife Mary gave birth to a baby boy, whom they named for the son their friends had lost. Benjamin Franklin would keep an eye on Francis Hopkinson, who would emerge as a leader of the new generation. The Franklins would not have another child themselves until the following decade when Sarah, or Sally, as they called her, was born. They had Sally inoculated when she was two.[45]

The issue of inoculation against smallpox brings together many aspects of the early years of Franklin's professional life in Philadelphia. Keimer's serialization of Chambers's *Cyclopaedia*, though not good journalism, did emphasize the growing desire among eighteenth-century readers to achieve an encyclopaedic level of knowledge. Franklin understood that information works best when it appeals to personal interest. Don't wait until the alphabet reaches 'I' to reprint an article about inoculation. Reprint it when people are threatened by smallpox. Given the public uncertainty about inoculation, a reprint from Chambers provided an objective opinion outside local controversy.

The amount of printed material was increasingly overwhelming. But Keimer's serialization of Chambers made the printed word more intimidating, not less. Franklin's careful selection of encyclopaedia articles to reprint shows his ability to decide what suited his subscribers. Franklin understood that his job as a journalist involved mediating the massive amount of available information and choosing the best and most useful articles for his readers.

3

The Improvement and Well-Peopling of the Colonies

What is Franklin up to now? So might anyone have wondered who walked past his busy shop during the winter of 1737–8 and heard all sorts of clanging and banging. Having purchased some steel plates, he was designing and constructing a new type of home-heating stove. By the next winter, he had begun selling his stoves to friends. As Franklin's need for steel increased, he had Robert Grace, now proprietor of Warwick Furnace, manufacture the steel plates. Grace also financed the publication of the pamphlet Franklin wrote to describe his new design, *An Account of the New Invented Pennsylvanian Fireplaces*.[1]

Part promotional tract and part scientific treatise, Franklin's pamphlet describes the stove's advantages. It improved upon the traditional fireplace, directing heat into the room, not up the chimney. It also conserved firewood and thus reduced fuel costs, the colonial homeowner's single biggest expense. Preventing sparks from flying up the chimney, the new stove minimized potential house fires. Franklin designed the front to open, letting people stare into the flames. To enhance its aesthetic appeal even more, he created an emblem for the top front plate: a smiling sun amid lush foliage. Its motto, *Alter idem*, echoes a Latin proverb, *Amicus est alter idem*, 'A friend is a second self.'

Franklin's pamphlet also discusses steel's strength and safety as a construction material. His portrayal of an iron foundry anticipates Thomas Hart Benton's mural *America Today*. Both celebrate the steelworker. In his *Account*, Franklin watches with fascination as the workmen pour out 'the flowing metal to cast large plates, and not the least smell of it to be perceived'.[2]

One source, J. T. Desaguliers's *Course of Experimental Philosophy*, bolsters Franklin's argument. Desaguliers heated an iron cube to a high temperature before drawing air through a hole in its centre to a receptacle holding a linnet, *Linaria cannabina*. The 'small bird', Franklin summarizes, 'breath'd that air without any inconvenience or suffering the least disorder'. Another linnet perished when exposed to the mephitis emanating from hot brass. Franklin concludes, 'Brass indeed stinks even when cold, and much more when hot; lead too, when hot, yields a very unwholesome steam; but iron is always sweet, and every way taken is wholesome and friendly to the human body – except in weapons.'[3]

Franklin's pamphlet gave his stove international renown. One day John Bartram showed him a Dutch translation that J. F. Gronovius had sent.[4] Bartram's correspondence with the Dutch botanist reflects his own international renown. Having learned botany from Breintnall and Logan, he surpassed them to become colonial America's greatest botanist. Breintnall had put Bartram in contact with Collinson, who arranged for him to collect plants for several European naturalists.

Franklin encouraged Bartram's botanical research. He raised funds to support the intrepid botanist's American travels, loaned him the latest scientific literature, gave him free access to the Library Company and, as Philadelphia postmaster, franked parcels containing Bartram's botanical specimens: an early American instance of the government subsidizing scientific research.

Bartram enjoyed their conversations. Franklin's facetious talk, he said, had the magical power of dispelling melancholy fumes and cheering the spirit. He also looked to Franklin for counsel. When his son William was searching for a career in the 1750s, Bartram

Franklin stove, *c*. 1795, cast iron.

asked for advice. Relating the episode to Collinson, he revealed
Franklin's deliberate manner. Before answering Bartram's question,
Franklin paused to ponder it. Breaking his lengthy silence, he said
William should become an engraver.[5]

Franklin reported a conversation they had after Oxford
professor Johann Jakob Dillenius sent Bartram some ground
liverwort, *Peltigera canina*, which supposedly cured rabies. Bartram
and Franklin compared the English specimen with the ground
liverwort native to Pennsylvania.[6] As the report suggests, the
comparative method was becoming an increasingly useful way to
study natural history.

Typically, Franklin encouraged others to pursue botany, but
he was responsible for introducing one European tree species to
America. He noticed an imported willow basket discarded in Dock
Creek one day. Its wood had begun to sprout, so he planted the
shoots in Isaac Norris's garden. The basket willow, *Salix viminalis*,

flourished, and consequently so did the American basket-making industry.[7]

In 1743 Bartram and Franklin planned a colonial scientific society. Franklin's *Proposal for Promoting Useful Knowledge among the British Plantations in America* named the group – the American Philosophical Society – and established its principles. Since the long stretch of land that formed colonial America extended through different geographical regions, it provided a natural laboratory for scientific research and offered diverse resources that could contribute to the improvement of the colonies. American 'virtuosi' – scientifically inclined gentlemen – needed an organization to coordinate their research. Franklin's wistful tone enhances his rhetoric: 'Many useful particulars remain uncommunicated, die with the discoverers, and are lost to mankind.'[8]

Travelling to New England in June 1743, the month after publishing his proposal, Franklin met Cadwallader Colden,

Frank Cousins, *John Bartram's House, 1731*, late 19th century, glass plate negative.

John Wollaston, *Cadwallader Colden*, 1749–52, oil on canvas.

who agreed to promote the proposed society. In Boston, Franklin attended Dr Archibald Spencer's scientific lectures. His autobiography thanks Spencer for introducing him to electrical research, but Franklin also encountered it elsewhere. Isaac Greenwood, who had previously assisted Desaguliers in London, was now an itinerant scientific lecturer, having been dismissed from Harvard for excessive drinking. Greenwood introduced many students to science. In 1740 Franklin had acted as his Philadelphia impresario and arranged for him to lecture at the Library Company.

In 1744 the American Philosophical Society elected Hopkinson president, Coleman treasurer and Franklin secretary. Bartram became the society's botanist, and Rhoads directed its mechanical studies. Dr Thomas Bond, whom Franklin knew from St John's Lodge and the Library Company, oversaw medicine. Despite their enthusiasm, the founding members could not sustain the society. Disappointed, Bartram said they could have made it work if more members had traded their time at the coffee-house or the chessboard for 'the curious amusements of natural observations'.[9] Two decades would pass before Bond and Rhoads revived the American Philosophical Society and re-established it on a permanent basis, electing Franklin president in absentia.

During the mid-1740s Franklin and Jared Eliot began a fruitful scientific correspondence. Eliot asked about hemp cultivation among Pennsylvania farmers, and Franklin told him they drained swamps to grow hemp, an idea Eliot would record in *Essays upon Field-Husbandry*. Franklin also told Eliot about the seashell fossils that Bartram had found in the mountains and donated to the Library Company for its cabinet of curiosities. These mountaintop seashells prompted Franklin to exclaim, ''Tis certainly the wreck of a world we live on!'[10]

Besides Bartram, Bond, Breintnall, Colden, Eliot, Hopkinson, Logan and Rhoads in America, Franklin's network of scientific friends in the mid-1740s included Collinson in England and Kalm in Sweden. Whitfield J. Bell observes, 'The many-sided genius of Benjamin Franklin included a rare talent for friendship. His friendships were in fact one of his memorable achievements.'[11] On 16 March 1746, Franklin's circle of friends contracted when Breintnall's body turned up on the New Jersey side of the Delaware River, the victim of an apparent suicide. Science was making the world more legible, but it could not plumb the depths of the soul. It still can't.

Nature echoes the names of Franklin's friends. Having discovered some new genera, Linnaeus called one genus

Bartramia, another *Coldenia*. Linnaeus named richweed *Collinsonia canadensis*. And *Fothergilla*, a genus of shrubbery in the witch hazel family native to the American South, honours Dr John Fothergill, a British physician and botanist whom Franklin would befriend. Upon learning about *Coldenia*, Franklin congratulated Colden for the immortality the scientific name gave him: 'No species or genus of plants was ever lost, or ever will be while the world continues; and therefore your name, now annext to one of them, will last forever.'[12]

Franklin's comment reflects a widely held concept: the great chain of being. Since God supposedly made the world complete and perfect, no species could ever become extinct. Nature linked together the entirety of creation. As Pope says in *An Essay on Man*, 'From Nature's chain whatever link you strike,/ Tenth or ten thousandth, breaks the chain alike.'[13] Some, including Franklin, would question the great chain of being, but the concept lasted through the mid-eighteenth century, a stumbling block that hindered natural history.

In 1745 Collinson presented the Library Company with a long glass tube and a pamphlet describing the electrical research of Swiss scientist Albrecht von Haller. Experimenters could rub the tube to generate the static electricity necessary to replicate Haller's experiments. The pamphlet is a ghost, meaning that no copies survive, but one lasted long enough to inspire Franklin's earliest electrical research. He had a local glass-blower make additional tubes, so others could experiment. Hopkinson, for one, discovered that pointed metal rods not only drew off, but threw off electricity.[14]

The following year Franklin learned about the Leyden jar, an electrical condenser made from a cork-stoppered glass bottle partly filled with water, with a wire pierced through the cork and dipped into the water. To charge the jar, an experimenter would touch the wire's exposed end to the conductor of an electrical machine.

A hand-cranked machine marked an improvement upon the glass tube, eliminating the tiresome rubbing. Leyden jars let Franklin broaden his experiments. For him, the summer of 1746 was the summer of electricity.

Others believed the Leyden jar stored the electricity that the machine created. Franklin hypothesized that the machine did not create electricity. Combined with the Leyden jar, the machine collected electricity that already existed. The amount of electricity stayed the same. The apparatus merely separated it into positive and negative charges. Franklin was the first to devise this theory and coin these terms.

How the Leyden jar worked was a mystery. Franklin solved it, discovering that the electricity was not so much inside the jar as on the glass. One did not need a Leyden jar to collect it. With an impish playfulness, Franklin collected electricity on the inside of a partly filled wine glass, which could shock the drinker's lips. He called this supercharged cocktail an 'electrified bumper'.[15]

Electricity could also be collected on a pane of glass. Aware the electric power of Leyden jars could be increased by connecting them in series, Franklin charged a set of eleven glass panes separated by lead plates. Its electrical charge was so powerful, it could burn a hole through a quire of paper thick enough to stop a bullet.

Describing the Leyden jar, early experimenters had adapted the language of firearms. Like a musket, the Leyden jar was 'charged'. When it sparked, it was 'fired'. Franklin carried over this diction. A coordinated group of artillery pieces was called a battery; Franklin called his glass-pane-and-lead-plate arrangement an 'electrical battery'. He thus gave the term its modern sense. Every time we replace a battery in an electronic device and align its positive and negative poles, we pay homage to Benjamin Franklin.

Anxious to find practical applications for electricity, Franklin invented an electrical wheel to use as a jack for turning a large fowl over a fire – a decided improvement. Usually, the roasting spit was attached to a wheel containing a turnspit dog, which ran inside its circumference and, through a chain-and-pulley system, turned the spit. During the 1740s Philadelphia retailer Henry Clark placed notices in Franklin's *Gazette* advertising 'dogs and wheels, much preferable to any jacks for roasting any joynt of meat'.[16] Franklin neither perfected nor marketed his electrical jack, but he deserves credit for the idea. Benjamin Franklin invented rotisserie chicken.

Though eager to continue his electrical experiments, Franklin set them aside in late 1747 when French privateers attacked ships and settlements on the Delaware River. In addition, French troops and their Native American allies attacked Pennsylvania's frontier settlements: the latest salvos in King George's War, as the American theatre of the War of the Austrian Succession is known. Committed to pacifism, the Quakers who controlled the Pennsylvania Assembly refused to authorize a militia to defend the colony.

In response, Franklin wrote *Plain Truth*, a call to arms revealing the danger they faced. Since their colony would not defend itself, Franklin urged Pennsylvanians to arm themselves. After publishing *Plain Truth* that November, he formed the Association, a colonial militia founded on democratic principles. The 'Associators' elected company officers, who, in turn, elected the higher officers. On 1 January 1748 the company officers elected Franklin their colonel. Pleading military inexperience, he refused the office, serving as a common soldier instead.

Regardless, Franklin remained the Association's de facto leader. He was, in Logan's words, 'the very soul of the whole'.[17] Franklin cherished the Association, involving himself in every aspect of it, down to designing company flags. His designs reveal Franklin's creativity, interest in iconography and egalitarianism. One flag depicts three arms, the hands joined by grasping the wrists of the others. Their different shirt sleeves – ruffles, plain linen, checked gingham – represent the three classes of colonial society: gentleman, merchant, artisan.[18]

Though they never had to battle their French and Indian enemies, the Associators struck fear into Thomas Penn. William Penn, the colony's founder, had overseen Pennsylvania with benevolent compassion; Thomas, his son and heir, who held a three-quarter stake in the proprietary colony, let greed be his guide. Richard Penn, who held the remainder, supported his older brother's administrative decisions. Both had abandoned their father's Quaker faith to smooth their way through English society. Thomas Penn saw anyone who endangered his income as a threat. He feared Franklin's leadership. Calling Franklin 'a dangerous man', Penn said, 'I should be very glad he inhabited any other country, as I believe him of a very uneasy spirit.'[19]

The Associators drifted apart once the Treaty of Aix-la-Chapelle ended the War of the Austrian Succession, but Franklin remained a local hero. The Association is an important precursor to the American Revolution. Working outside the structure of the British colonial government, the Associators defended the lives and rights of colonial Americans, whose safety was being ignored by those in power.

The date of 1 January 1748, the day the company officers held their election, was also the day Franklin retired to devote himself to scientific research and civic affairs. He would soon turn 42. While retiring from full-time involvement with his printing business, he still put much work into the *Pennsylvania Gazette*. In addition, he remained the leading wholesale distributor for American paper and continued the lowly task of collecting rags for the papermakers.[20]

Franklin had positioned himself well prior to retirement. Four years earlier he had learned that London printer and bookseller William Strahan had a favourite journeyman, David Hall, who wanted to emigrate. Franklin welcomed Hall to Philadelphia. After his arrival in 1745, Franklin made him shop foreman. Hall also imported books from Strahan to expand their retail trade. Once Franklin retired, he made Hall a partner and turned the shop over to him.[21]

The number of public offices Franklin filled is astonishing. On 4 October 1748 he was elected to city council. The following year, he was named a justice of the peace. Through the 1740s he continued serving as clerk of the Pennsylvania Assembly, but on 9 May 1751 he was elected to the Assembly. Isaac Norris, its speaker, could always count on Franklin. During his time as an assemblyman, no one chaired or served on more committees.

Franklin effectively threaded his way through the mazy colonial politics. Pennsylvania had two major political parties, the proprietary party, which supported the Penns, and the Quaker or anti-proprietary party. There was a split among the Quakers. Some were pacifists while others advocated military defence. Franklin sided with the non-pacifist Quakers but never officially belonged to either political party. His numerous legislative accomplishments testify to his hard work and personal charisma.

Two essays Franklin contributed to the *Gazette* in 1751 respond to an insensitive report by the Board of Trade, the advisory body overseeing colonial affairs. As Britain transported more and more felons to Pennsylvania, the Assembly passed a series of acts limiting convict transportation. The Board of Trade advised the Privy Council to disallow the legislation because transported felons 'might be of publick utility, in the improvement and well peopling of the said province'.[22]

That year, felons swept across Maryland and Pennsylvania on a violent rampage. In April Franklin catalogued their crime spree in 'On Transported Felons', asking, 'In what can Britain show a more sovereign contempt for us, than by emptying their gaols into our settlements; unless they would likewise empty their jakes on our tables!' The word 'jakes' was a colloquial term for privy or outhouse. Franklin's scatological imagery vividly illustrates the widespread colonial anger with the British practice of sending convicted criminals to America. Many British and colonial newspapers reprinted the article. The *London Evening Post*, to take one previously unrecorded reprint as an example, excerpted 'On Transported Felons'.[23]

Franklin returned to the subject in May with 'Rattlesnakes for Felons', a modest proposal suggesting that since Britain transported criminals to America, America should transport rattlesnakes to Britain. His sarcasm is palpable:

> What is a little housebreaking, shoplifting, or highway robbing; what is a son now and then corrupted and hang'd, a daughter debauch'd and pox'd, a wife stabb'd, a husband's throat cut, or a child's brains beat out with an axe, compar'd with this 'improvement and well peopling of the colonies!'[24]

The Board of Trade's term 'improvement' especially irked Franklin. Few words are more central to his civic affairs or, indeed, his outlook on life. He was always doing what he could to improve Philadelphia, to improve the health, welfare, safety and intellectual lives of its citizens and, more and more, of humanity in general. Franklin was shocked that the British administrators were so ignorant, so callous, so totally out of touch that they imagined convicts would improve the colonies.

Franklin also wrote 'Observations Concerning the Increase of Mankind' in 1751. He downplayed the work, calling it 'a small paper of thoughts on the peopling of countries'. What Lemay calls it reveals the work's profound significance. It is 'the fundamental document of the American Revolution'. Without advocating American independence, 'Observations' does anticipate it. This groundbreaking demographic study argues convincingly that North America would surpass England to become the most populous and important part of the British Empire.[25]

Basically, Franklin observes that people marry and have children when they can afford to and that the American frontier would let them acquire land, start their own farms and prosper. Franklin initially circulated this demographic essay in manuscript. Once he sent a copy to England, Collinson urged him to publish it, which he did in 1755. Reprinted numerous times thereafter, 'Observations' would influence Thomas Malthus and Adam Smith.[26]

Franklin involved himself in practically every improvement project in Philadelphia during the mid-eighteenth century. In 1749 he wrote *Proposals Relating to the Education of Youth in Pennsylvania*, the founding document of the Philadelphia Academy (now, University of Pennsylvania). Franklin set forth a subscription to raise funds, wrote the school's constitution, oversaw construction and recruited faculty. He appointed Charles Thomson to be a Latin and Greek tutor. The appointment acknowledged Thomson's classical expertise and established a lifelong friendship. The constitution's first sentence emphasizes the school's value to posterity: 'Nothing can more effectually contribute to the cultivation and improvement of a country, the wisdom, riches, and strength, virtue and piety, the welfare and happiness of a people, than a proper education of youth.'[27]

Franklin was elected president at the first meeting of the board of trustees. Despite his leadership, he could not convince the other trustees to accept his curriculum. Franklin had planned a radical new programme of study, one that did not require students to know Greek or Latin. If he had had his way, courses and readings would be in English, and students would have the opportunity to customize their coursework with electives. He also advocated a physical fitness programme. The other trustees insisted on a standard classical curriculum. When Philadelphia Academy officially opened on 7 January 1751, Franklin was proud to see Francis Hopkinson in its first class. Sadly, Thomas Hopkinson would not live to see his son graduate. He succumbed to illness on 5 November 1751.

Thomas Bond hoped to establish a hospital in Philadelphia, which would be the first in colonial America, but his subscription campaign could not gain any traction. Practically everyone he approached asked whether he had consulted Franklin, whose name by now was synonymous with community improvement. Bond took the hint and contacted Franklin, who was happy to help.

Franklin devised an innovative scheme. He asked the Pennsylvania Assembly for support but promised the legislature it would only have to donate matching funds if he and Bond could privately raise £2,000. The legislators accepted the idea, never imagining Bond and Franklin could raise that much. The promise of matching funds helped them reach the required amount, so the legislators had to pony up. Current businesses that match individual donations follow a strategy of charitable giving that Franklin invented.

Once the Pennsylvania Hospital was organized, its founders converted a Philadelphia mansion for temporary use until a proper hospital could be erected. The temporary facility opened in February 1752. The cornerstone of the new building was laid in

Robert Scot, *The Pennsylvania Hospital*, engraving, *c.* 1790.

1755, the year Franklin was elected hospital president. Rhoads, who sat on the board with Bond and Franklin, designed the building, oversaw its construction and personally helped the workmen.[28] On 17 December 1756 it admitted its first patient. The Pennsylvania Hospital thrives today, another monument to Franklin's philanthropic spirit.

Franklin periodically reported his electrical experiments to Collinson, who read his letters to the Royal Society. Its electricians largely dismissed Franklin's early theories, and its *Philosophical Transactions* rarely published his research. When Collinson reported Franklin's hypothesis that thunder and lightning were electrical phenomena, the Royal Society electricians just laughed.

Given the Society's reluctance to publish Franklin's research, Collinson and Fothergill collected, edited and published Franklin's letters independently. They arranged with Edward Cave, the publisher of the *Gentleman's Magazine*, to issue the book based on his research. While *Experiments and Observations on Electricity* was in press, Cave published a teaser in the May *Gentleman's Magazine*: the 2 March 1750 letter from Franklin to Collinson that proposed the use of lightning rods – the first published description of this modern safety device.[29]

Once Franklin understood that lightning was electricity, but before proving his hypothesis, he recognized the awesome power in his hands. In late 1751 he wrote to Colden:

> There are no bounds (but what expence and labour give) to the force man may raise and use in the electric way: for bottle may be added to bottle in infinitum, and all united and discharg'd together as one, the force and effect proportion'd to their number and size. The greatest known effects of common lightning, may, I think, without much difficulty be exceeded in this way: which a few years since could not have been believed, and even now may seem to many a little extravagant

to suppose. So we are got beyond the skill of Rabelais's devils of two year old, who, he humorously says, had only learnt to thunder and lighten a little round the head of a cabbage.[30]

Franklin refers to a minor episode late in *Gargantua and Pantagruel* in which Rabelais mentions a baby devil, who 'could not yet write or read, or hail and thunder, unless it were on parsly or colworts'.[31] The reference verifies Franklin's knowledge of Rabelais, but also conveys electricity's immense potential. Traditionally, lightning was an instrument of gods or devils, but humans could now harness a source of power that rivalled the heavens.

French researchers performed the experiment Franklin recommended to prove that lightning was electricity. Before learning about the French success, Franklin devised a simpler, but more dramatic experiment to prove his hypothesis. All he needed was a kite and a key. Uncertain of its success, Franklin had not communicated the idea beforehand, nor did he write it up afterwards. Stories of the experiment circulated orally throughout America and Europe, but Joseph Priestley's account in his *History of Electricity*, based on conversations with Franklin, is the sole source for reliable information about the kite experiment.[32]

During an electrical storm one night, Franklin and his son took a kite to an open field and sent it into the sky. Contrary to what popular culture says, the kite was not struck by lightning, which could have killed Franklin. As a positively charged storm cloud came in contact with a negatively charged one, they released electricity. The threads of Franklin's hempen kite string stood erect, showing the string was electrified. Franklin put his knuckle near the key he had dangling from the string and, sure enough, it threw a spark. Soon he had collected copious amounts of electricity with a Leyden jar.

The kite experiment practically elevated Franklin to godlike status. Having stolen the celestial fire, he was the new Prometheus.

Henry S. Sadd, after John Ludlow Morton, *The Philosopher and His Kite*, mezzotint, 1840. This popular image depicts Benjamin Franklin's son William as a chubby-cheeked boy. In reality, William Franklin was around 23 years old at the time of the kite experiment.

The Royal Society readily published his subsequent research and, in 1753, awarded him its highest honour, the Copley Medal. Three years later, it elected him a fellow. Throughout Europe and America, lightning rods sprouted from public buildings, churches and homes. Constructing his home atop a mountain, Thomas Jefferson used a lightning rod to protect Monticello. After one fierce electrical storm, he said, 'If it hadn't been for that Franklin the whole house would have gone.'[33]

Though Franklin's electrical research represents his greatest contribution to science, he never limited himself to one field of study. Besides astronomy, botany, meteorology and mineralogy, he also studied geography and navigation. He was intrigued with the possibility of finding the chimerical Northwest Passage. His interest was both scientific and economic. He knew that discovering a trade route atop North America would boost the colonial economy. He obtained several books on the subject to broaden his knowledge and considered the feasibility of another expedition.

Reading *A Vindication of the Conduct of Captain Christopher Middleton*, Franklin encountered a familiar name: John Wigate. Wigate had stayed in London when Franklin returned to Philadelphia but had little success as a printer. *The Breeches, A Tale*, a rollicking verse satire, is the only known book he published. In 1741 Wigate joined Middleton as clerk aboard the naval sloop *Furnace*. Once the ship's search for the Northwest Passage had failed, Wigate joined Arthur Dobbs to smear Middleton. Wigate's greatest claim to fame is the 1746 map he issued, which shows the 'Wager Strait' leading from Hudson Bay westwards. Another expedition discovered that the 'Wager Strait' was not a strait, but a closed bay, just as Middleton had said.[34]

Franklin raised £1,500 to obtain and equip a schooner to find the Northwest Passage. Named after the ship Jason sailed to find the Golden Fleece, the *Argo* set sail on 4 March 1753. Its search was unsuccessful, but Franklin was undaunted. Some investors pulled out, but he raised additional funds to finance a second voyage of the *Argo,* which also failed. Franklin's Argonauts did not return empty-handed. They brought back several indigenous artefacts for the Library Company's cabinet of curiosities.

Ambitious and indefatigable, Franklin accepted more responsibilities. Having served as Philadelphia postmaster since 1737, he set his sights on the post office's top colonial job, Postmaster General of North America. In 1751 he solicited Collinson's help and began campaigning for the position. Two years later, Franklin was named joint Postmaster General with Williamsburg printer, newspaper editor and postmaster William Hunter.[35]

Post office business let Franklin travel throughout colonial America, inspecting postal routes and researching possible locations for new post offices. Hunter came to Philadelphia, so they could begin their work together. In early January 1754 they travelled through Pennsylvania and Maryland. Near Virginia, they parted company. Hunter returned to Williamsburg, and Franklin headed north, reaching Annapolis on Tuesday 22 January, just in time to attend a meeting of the Tuesday Club of Annapolis at Dr Alexander Hamilton's home.

The founder of the Tuesday Club, Hamilton kept the club records, which he expanded into its history. Though Franklin was a member of several clubs, none had recording secretaries. Consequently, Hamilton's writings provide a unique glimpse into Franklin's social behaviour while attending a club whose well-educated members enjoyed good food, good drink and good jokes. Given the liberties Hamilton took with *The History of the Tuesday Club*, the ensuing dialogue follows the club records.[36]

The night that Franklin attended, deputy president William Lux – or, to use his club name, Crinkum Crankum – presided, and John Beale Bordley – Quirpum Comic – was master of ceremonies. Bordley could assume an air so serious it put others in stitches. Jonas Green, the Annapolis printer known in the club as Jonathan Grog, also attended. Franklin knew him as both the editor of the *Maryland Gazette* and the Annapolis postmaster. Hamilton wrote a vivid pen portrait of Green: 'His body is thick and well set, and for one of his make and stature he had a good sizeable belly, into which he loves much to convey the best vittles and drink.' Hamilton aptly named himself 'Loquacious Scribble' and called Franklin 'Electro Vitrifice', a name that sounds slightly onanistic: it means electric glass-rubber.[37]

Franklin's club name reveals Hamilton's familiarity with his electrical research. The club also knew him as a wit. In 1747 Green had published his brilliant hoax, 'The Speech of Miss Polly Baker', which presents what is purportedly the courtroom speech of a woman who had been seduced and abandoned before turning to

Dr Alexander Hamilton of Annapolis, *Loquacious Scribble*, self-portrait, pen and ink wash drawing, from the manuscript 'The History of the Ancient and Honorable Tuesday Club: From the Earliest Ages down to this Present Year', *c.* 1755.

prostitution and giving birth to five healthy babies out of wedlock. Justifying her life choices, her speech ridicules straight-laced Christian morality. Polly Baker is so convincing that she persuades the presiding judge to marry her.

The club planned a mock trial for 22 January. It pretended Quirpum Comic had stolen the president's chair to sell piecemeal but could not sell its leather seat because, to repeat Hamilton's traditional simile, it 'smelt like a fox'. (In American culture, the striped skunk, which Linnaeus named after the god of pestilential smells – *Mephitis mephitis* – would replace the fox as the proverbial stinker.) Loquacious Scribble argued that Quirpum Comic should be demoted from the rank of long-standing member.

'Why Mr Secretary', Jonathan Grog responded, 'you would not have us to dock the gentleman. I suppose his member, however it may stand now at this juncture is as long as ever.'

'Ha, ha, ha', laughed Crinkum Crankum. 'The longstanding members I think are waggish.'

'Longstanding members', Electro Vitrifice interjected, obviously unable to resist. 'Longstanding members, I think gentlemen, with submission, are not so properly waggish, because if they stand they cannot wag.'

By 1 February Franklin was back in Philadelphia for the latest session of the Pennsylvania Assembly. The next month, who should show up at his doorstep but Quirpum Comic. Bordley's arrival provided welcome relief to the increasingly tense legislative proceedings. He recorded a snippet from a conversation with Franklin. A great agricultural experimenter, Bordley studied the latest research. So did Franklin. After receiving Eliot's *Essay upon Field-Husbandry*, Franklin offered the book to some Pennsylvania farmers, who turned it down. Franklin told Bordley what they had said: 'We want no information on husbandry, we know all about it – Give us labour, we want not your books of information.'[38]

Once Quirpum Comic left, Quirpum Tragic arrived. Or, to drop the figurative language, less than two months after Bordley visited Franklin, a letter from George Washington reached Philadelphia, reporting that the French had captured the partly finished British fort near present-day Pittsburgh and begun erecting Fort Duquesne, which would let them control the Ohio River and make it easier to attack Pennsylvania's frontier settlements. The French and Indian War, as the American theatre of the Seven Years War would become known, had yet to be declared, but skirmishes on the Pennsylvania frontier anticipated it.

Franklin knew intercolonial cooperation would provide the best defence. In the 9 May 1754 *Pennsylvania Gazette*, he published 'Join or Die', the first American newspaper cartoon and the earliest symbol of colonial American unity. The cartoon depicts a snake cut into parts, each representing a different colonial American region. Franklin's iconic snake reflects a prevalent impulse in American culture, the use of indigenous creatures from the wilderness as totems of power. Tracing its cultural history, Daniel Royot argues that Franklin's snake would evolve into the burlesque *Homo americanus*, the tall-talking half-horse, half-alligator braggart of the American folk tradition.[39]

The cut-snake cartoon was not the only sign pointing towards colonial American unification. The Albany Conference, which was held the month after the cartoon appeared, brought Franklin together with delegates from several other colonies. Influenced by his friend Archibald Kennedy, New York's receiver general, Franklin drafted 'The Albany Plan of Union'. The conference approved Franklin's plan, but the colonial legislatures rejected it. The cut-snake icon endured in the popular memory. When French troops forced Washington to surrender Fort Necessity in July, Hunter reported what had happened in the *Virginia Gazette*, after which he editorialized about the humiliating defeat – hoping it would change the minds of those against colonial unification and 'inforce a late ingenious emblem well worthy of their attention and consideration'.[40]

Post office business took Benjamin and William Franklin, now Philadelphia postmaster, to Annapolis in April 1755. Their timing prevented them from attending the Tuesday Club, but they had a chance to see Jonas Green again. They also met Colonel Benjamin Tasker, whom Franklin had befriended in Albany. Tasker invited them to his plantation. The Franklins accepted.

Cresting a ridge on the road to Tasker's, they could see a whirlwind in the valley below. As the others watched it, Franklin spurred his horse to chase it. History seldom portrays Franklin on horseback, but he was a good rider. Once he started, his son had trouble keeping pace. The difference between a whirlwind and a tornado is a matter of scale: a tornado is a major whirlwind. What Franklin observed was not a tornado, but it seems close enough to earn him another first: Benjamin Franklin is the first storm chaser.

Aware of traditional beliefs about breaking whirlwinds, Franklin tried breaking this one by striking his whip through it. Cracking his whip while chasing the whirlwind, Franklin resembles the avenging angel in Joseph Addison's poem 'The Campaign'. He 'rides in the whirlwind, and directs the storm'.[41] Or, to use a character from the American tall tale tradition, Franklin prefigures Pecos Bill, who leaps onto an Oklahoma tornado and rides it clear across the Southwest. More prudent than Pecos Bill, Franklin backed away from the whirlwind as its girth increased. Watching it pass through a stand of large trees, he saw it snap off some sizeable branches and understood how foolish his attempt to break the whirlwind had been.

Reporting the episode to Collinson, Franklin included some dialogue. Upon rejoining Tasker, he wondered if whirlwinds were common in Maryland.

'No, not at all common,' Tasker replied, 'but we got this on purpose to treat Mr Franklin.'

Benjamin Franklin, *Join or Die*, woodcut, 1754. Appearing in the 9 May 1754 issue of the *Pennsylvania Gazette*, this, the first political cartoon in the history of American journalism, exhorts the British American colonies to unite against the French and their Native American allies during the Seven Years War.

'And a very high treat it was,' Franklin concluded.

The Franklins continued to Winchester, Virginia, to establish a new post office there before reaching Frederick, Maryland, in the third week of April to discuss military postal service with General Edward Braddock, the new commander of British forces in North America.

Since Braddock was disappointed with the colonial support he had received so far, Franklin introduced him to Pennsylvania politics, describing the conflict arising from the pacifist Quaker legislators and a governor who could neither think nor act for himself. Franklin promised to supply Braddock with what he needed. In a herculean effort, he persuaded hundreds of Pennsylvania farmers to provide wagons and horses for Braddock's march. He also convinced them to drive the wagons but said they would not have to fight. In addition, he personally guaranteed the farmers against loss.

As Braddock and his troops neared Fort Duquesne in early July, George Washington, then serving as his aide, warned that the French fought differently in America than in Europe and recommended they attack Indian-style. Braddock ignored his advice. Washington offered to lead the provincial troops separately. Braddock scorned the offer. On 9 July 1755 Braddock led the British and colonial troops to slaughter. During the Battle of the Monongahela, as it became known, French troops and their Indian allies ambushed the much larger British forces, killing hundreds of troops, including many officers. Braddock himself was mortally wounded. Washington, who had two horses shot from under him, escaped unwounded and led the survivors to safety.

Fothergill, who was the London correspondent from the English Friends' Yearly Meeting to the Philadelphia Yearly Meeting, advised the pacifist Quakers to resign from the Assembly during the war before the Privy Council forced them out because of their opposition to military service. The pacifist Quakers – the 'stiffrumps', Franklin called them – mostly took Fothergill's advice. The following year, Franklin reported to Collinson: 'All the stiffrumps except one, that could be suspected of opposing the service from religious motives, have voluntarily quitted the Assembly.'[42]

During Franklin's tenure as an assemblyman, Pennsylvania went through several governors. All puppets of the proprietors, they acted under secret instructions forbidding them to approve any bills levying taxes on proprietary lands. The Penns also refused to contribute to other colonial expenses, not even ones that materially benefitted them, such as Indian treaties.

In November 1755, after the governor vetoed the Assembly's latest military spending bill, Norris appointed Franklin to a committee to answer the veto. Franklin's report emphasizes that the legislators had done all they could, given the Penns' restrictions, which effectively prevented the governor from approving any military spending bills. The legislature had taken every step possible, short of violating the rights of Pennsylvania citizens. Concluding the report, Franklin wrote a sentence that Americans would quote time and again when faced with balancing national security and civil liberty: 'Those who would give up essential liberty, to purchase a little temporary safety, deserve neither liberty nor safety.'[43]

After the Battle of the Monongahela, the British troops fled to Philadelphia, leaving the Pennsylvania frontier undefended. In late November 1755 Franklin drafted a bill to establish a voluntary militia. The Assembly passed the bill, and the governor approved it. Unlike the Association, this new militia had legal standing, but it, too, was based on democratic principles, letting the militiamen elect their leaders.

Before the militia could be organized, frontier violence demanded swift action. In late November, Philadelphia received word that a Shawnee war party had attacked Gnadenhütten, a Moravian mission village 75 miles (120 km) northwest. The Shawnee killed everyone who did not escape into the woods and torched the village. On 5 January 1756 the governor appointed Franklin military and civilian commander of the Pennsylvania frontier. With his son, William, as his aide, Franklin led five hundred troops into the wilderness.

Located on the opposite side of Lehigh Gap, Gnadenhütten's strategic location gave the French and their Native American allies a stronghold from which to launch attacks. Lehigh Gap was a narrow pass through the Blue Mountains. Rocks overhung the road on either side, letting a small party inflict massive casualties onto any who dared ascend the pass. On 10 January 1756 William Franklin led the Pennsylvania troops through the gap unscathed. On the opposite side, they found a scene of unimaginable horror, the dead bodies of men, women and children decaying in the streets of Gnadenhütten.

Benjamin Franklin and his men buried the dead and built a stockade, thus giving Gnadenhütten's survivors renewed hope. After Franklin had secured the village, the governor unexpectedly recalled the Pennsylvania Assembly. Leaving an experienced officer in charge, he and William returned to Philadelphia. When the company officers elected Benjamin Franklin colonel in February, he accepted the command. Colonel Franklin did not serve for long. The Privy Council disallowed the militia bill, seeing it as much too democratic.

Before the Privy Council quashed the Pennsylvania militia, Colonel Franklin had the chance to inspect his troops. On 18 March his men staged an elaborate and highly choreographed procession, complete with light artillery, heavy artillery, cavalry and music. Musicians on drum, fife and oboe marched with the troops. This was another Franklin first: these musicians formed the first band in American military history and thus established an important military tradition.[44]

When the procession reached Franklin's door, the men discharged their small arms and their cannon. Though flattered, Franklin found all this pomp a little silly. Thomas Penn did not. Learning about a parade in Franklin's honour, Penn had a conniption fit. No one had ever given him a parade. Franklin's version of the event reflects his mixed feelings: 'The first time I review'd my regiment, they accompanied me to my house, and would salute me with some rounds fired before my door, which shook down and broke several glasses of my electrical apparatus.'[45]

Perhaps no episode better summarizes the situation Franklin faced during the Seven Years War. His desire to pursue scientific research clashed with his responsibility to Pennsylvania. Longing to resume his research, he could not do so while the war persisted and lives were at risk. Franklin put responsibility for fellow citizens above devotion to science. After all, he could not improve people's lives unless he saved them first.

4

An American Agent in London

As the French and Indian War persisted, Pennsylvania proprietors Thomas and Richard Penn still refused to let the Pennsylvania Assembly tax their lands, lands the colonists were risking their lives to defend. Before January 1757 had ended, the Pennsylvania Assembly had had enough. It resolved that two representatives, Isaac Norris and Benjamin Franklin, visit London on its behalf. Norris's poor health kept him home, but Franklin agreed to travel wherever his fellow legislators wished.

He hoped to take his family, but Deborah, deathly afraid of crossing the ocean, refused. She would stay home with Sally, now thirteen, to manage their business affairs. William would accompany his father, as would two young slaves, Peter and King. It is hard to reconcile Franklin the defender of freedom with Franklin the slaveholder. Time would change his mind. Late in life, he would become an ardent abolitionist, finding slavery 'an atrocious debasement of human nature'. Besides chronicling Franklin's shifting attitude towards slavery, historians have the responsibility to reconstruct, as much as possible, the lives of his slaves. Benjamin, William, Peter and King boarded the *General Wall* in New York on 5 June 1757.[1]

In the naval convoy, Franklin noticed that the sea was smooth behind two ships, choppy behind others. He asked Captain Walter Lutwidge what it meant. Struggling to get his ship to speed, Lutwidge was in no mood for conversation. 'The cooks', he snapped, emptied 'their greasy water thro' the scuppers, which has greased the sides of those ships a little'. This episode inspired Franklin's experiments with oil to still water.[2]

Lutwidge suspected his ship's cargo was slowing it down. The front of the vessel seemed too heavy. As an experiment – 'This is the age of experiments,' Franklin proclaimed as he related this story – Lutwidge had everyone come aft. The packet quickly accelerated, thus confirming his suspicion. Once his crew reorganized the hold, the *General Wall* proved the fastest in the fleet.[3]

Near Nantucket the convoy turned towards Nova Scotia, leaving the *General Wall* to continue alone. Confident his speed would keep them safe, Lutwidge boasted the *General* could do 13 knots and dared anyone to bet otherwise. Archibald Kennedy Jr fellow passenger and son of Franklin's New York friend, took the bet. An officer in the royal navy, Kennedy 'heaved the log' to measure the speed. To his surprise, the *General Wall*, sure enough, was doing 13 knots. Though happy to take Kennedy's money, Lutwidge was playing for higher stakes. In wartime, he bet his life on its speed. Several times French privateers pursued them, but the *General Wall* escaped them all.

While Lutwidge was asleep in his bunk Saturday night, 16 July, something went horribly wrong as they approached the Isles of Scilly. No one saw the lighthouse until midnight, when the *General Wall* was almost on top of it. Kennedy woke up and barked out a command, 'Wear round, all sails standing!' The men brought the vessel on the other tack, turning its head around. This manoeuvre endangered the masts but saved the ship. When the *General Wall* passed Scilly Point, its captain remained at deep cover.

A dense morning fog masked the Cornish coast. Around 9 o'clock the fog, in Franklin's words, 'lifted up from the water like the curtain at a play house, discovering underneath the town of Falmouth, the vessels in its harbour, and the fields that surrounded it'. Coming ashore Sunday morning, they heard church bells.

Franklin wrote to Deborah: 'Were I a Roman Catholic, perhaps I should on this occasion vow to build a chapel to some saint; but as I am not, if I were to vow at all, it should be to build a lighthouse.'[4]

From Falmouth they travelled to London. Stonehenge was the highlight of their overland journey. What was it? A monument? An observatory? A temple? How could its builders have moved these massive blocks? Stonehenge was one mystery beyond Franklin's puzzle-solving abilities. Late Tuesday night, 26 July, they entered London and found lodgings at the Bear at Bridgefoot.

The next morning Benjamin and William Franklin crossed London Bridge to explore the city. The bridge looked much different than it had three decades earlier. The pikes holding the severed heads of traitors had disappeared, and the houses and shops lining either side of the bridge were being torn down. With their removal, London would lose one of its most iconic sights.

William Strahan and Peter Collinson were two Londoners Franklin especially wanted to see. Years earlier, he and Strahan had begun a business correspondence that had warmed into a friendship. Collinson lived and worked at the Red Lion on the opposite side of London Bridge. He had much advice for the sightseers, having explored London's nooks and crannies and searched for survivals from antiquity while admiring its latest buildings.[5]

The Franklins found more permanent lodgings at 7 Craven Street, a five-minute walk from Whitehall. Margaret Stevenson, the widow who ran the boarding house, was Franklin's age, and they got along well. He also befriended her daughter Polly, who would leave London for Essex to care for her ailing aunt. Polly's absence let her develop a scientific correspondence with Franklin, who thought she would make an ideal daughter-in-law.

William Franklin hoped for a better match than the daughter of a boarding house widow. Before he found one, a dalliance resulted in an unplanned pregnancy. His son William Temple Franklin would be born in 1760. Unlike his father, William refused to raise his illegitimate son and placed Temple with a foster mother.

Before entering British society, the Franklins visited a peruke maker. Something of a dandy, William took pleasure in perukes. His father hated wearing one but accepted it as a necessary annoyance. At 51, he was too old for a brown peruke. Besides, the grizzles were more fashionable. William preferred a tie-wig, but his father chose a full-bottomed grizzle that covered his ears and lent dignity to his diplomatic work.[6]

Looking out his Craven Street window one morning, Franklin noticed a frail woman sweeping with a birch broom. Who could have hired her? 'Nobody,' she replied when he asked. 'But I am very poor and in distress, and I sweeps before gentlefolkeses doors, and hopes they will give me something.' Franklin promised her a shilling to sweep the whole street. When she returned three hours later, he could hardly believe she had finished, so he sent Peter to double-check. Peter walked up to the Strand and down to the Thames and saw that, sure enough, she had swept Craven Street clean. This old woman inspired Franklin's plan to remedy London's dusty streets. He drafted a proposal for street cleaning, which he presented to Fothergill, 'a great promoter of useful projects'.[7]

Franklin also sought advice concerning his official business. Approach the Penns directly, Fothergill advised. They might be willing to settle their differences with the Assembly without fuss or publicity. Alternatively, Collinson recommended that Franklin contact the president of the Privy Council, John Carteret, 2nd Earl Granville. In early August Franklin followed Collinson's advice.

'You Americans have wrong ideas of the nature of your constitution,' Granville told Franklin when they met at Whitehall. 'You contend that the king's instructions to his governors are not laws, and think yourselves at liberty to disregard them at your own discretion.' Those instructions, he continued, are 'the law of the land; for the king is the legislator of the colonies'.[8]

Benjamin Wilson, *Benjamin Franklin*, 1757–8, oil on canvas.

Astonished by Granville's ignorance, Franklin explained the colonial legislative process to him. Laws are made by the assemblies of each colony and presented to the king for his royal assent. Upon granting his assent, the king could neither repeal nor alter the laws. Much as the assemblies could not make permanent laws without the king's assent, the king could not make a law for the colonies without their assent. Granville said Franklin could not be more wrong.

After the disappointing encounter with Granville, Franklin reverted to Fothergill's advice and met the proprietors at Thomas

Penn's Spring Garden mansion. As Franklin enumerated the Pennsylvania Assembly's complaints to Thomas and Richard Penn, it became obvious that their position and his were nearly irreconcilable. Unbeknownst to Franklin, they had already taken steps to undermine his diplomatic mission.

The proprietors devised a strategy to handle the shrewd and stubborn man representing the Assembly. Pretending that Franklin might sway them, they asked him to submit his complaints in writing. He consulted a report from the Assembly's legislative committee to draft 'Heads of Complaint'. The Penns forwarded this document to their attorney, Ferdinando John Paris. During his time as clerk for the Assembly, Franklin had corresponded with Paris and found him arrogant and inflexible.

The Penns counted on Paris's unscrupulous behaviour. He advised them to submit the 'Heads of Complaint' to the attorney general, a step guaranteed to slow the process almost to a halt. Franklin could tell his political mission would take months, if not years. Recognizing him as their colony's shrewdest and strongest leader, the Penns knew the longer they kept him in London, the less trouble he could make in Pennsylvania. The lengthy political wrangling did benefit Franklin in one way: it gave him time to enjoy London's intellectual life.

Franklin became active with many London organizations. Already a fellow of the Royal Society, he could now attend its meetings and enjoy the camaraderie of Britain's leading scientists. A corresponding member of the Society of Arts, he could now attend its meetings, too. Also known as the Premium Society, this organization rewarded people for new ideas in developing industrial arts. Franklin also became active with London's Grand Lodge of the Masons.

While in London, Franklin would be elected to the Associates of the Late Dr Bray, an organization that sought to ameliorate the condition of slaves in America. His active participation with the Bray

Associates marks the first major shift in Franklin's attitude towards slavery. Speaking with other members, Franklin acknowledged the importance of establishing 'Negro schools'. Though it may seem ironic that Franklin still owned a slave while he advocated on behalf of ameliorating slavery, Peter's willingness to learn may have helped Franklin understand the possibility of educating slaves. Franklin's educational ideas impressed the Bray Associates, who would elect him chair one year and re-elect him the next.

Franklin attended his first meeting of the Society of Arts on 7 September 1757, but his attention to the other organizations would have to wait because he was soon struck with a serious illness. Troubled by intermittent fever and excruciating headaches, he would be confined to Craven Street for weeks. Fothergill shifted from political advisor to personal physician; Margaret Stevenson went from landlady to nurse; and Peter went from body servant to factotum, developing a thorough knowledge of London while running errands.

On 12 November the aurora borealis was visible from London. Franklin's failure to observe it suggests that illness continued to restrict his activities. Afterwards, he spoke with several British friends about the phenomenon, and John Bartram wrote to inform him that the northern lights had been visible from Philadelphia on the same night. The aurora borealis intrigued Franklin. Two decades later, he would draft a paper on the subject to be read at the Royal Academy of Sciences in Paris.[9]

Franklin's contacts in London's scientific community led to many new friendships. Dr John Pringle, whose study of epidemiology and the prevention of cross-infection remains a landmark in the history of medicine, became his best friend in London. They loved playing chess, but scientific inquiry sometimes took precedence: Pringle would take their pulse as they played. In a previously unrecorded anecdote, Richard Twiss, the author of an eighteenth-century chess handbook, said that Franklin and Pringle 'used frequently to play at chess together; and towards the end of the game, the physician discovered, that the velocity of his own as well as his adversary's pulse was considerably increased'.[10]

Discussing the power and potential of electricity with Franklin, Pringle asked about its therapeutic value. Franklin had attempted to treat several Philadelphians suffering from physical ailments. Some improved, but Franklin doubted electrotherapy was the cause. He told Pringle their improvement more likely stemmed from the exercise they got coming to his home regularly – either that or their powers of imagination. The placebo effect, as it is known today, was known in Franklin's time as 'cure by expectation', not, as it is sometimes mislabelled, 'cure by expectoration'. Patients who expected the cure to work imagined the cure had worked.[11]

Clubs gave Franklin more friends. He joined two dinner clubs. One met on Mondays, and the other on Thursdays. The Monday club gathered at the George and Vulture. John Ellicott, a professional watchmaker and amateur astronomer, was its driving force. Ingham Foster, an ironmonger with a fine personal library and a fossil-filled cabinet, had much in common with Franklin. Captain James Cook was another member. His South Sea voyages were partly planned on Monday nights around a table at the George and Vulture.[12]

Franklin's Thursday club initially met at St Paul's Coffeehouse but later switched to the London Coffeehouse, Ludgate Hill. The club did not have a formal name, but Franklin retrospectively called it the Club of Honest Whigs. Soon after reaching London, he met John Canton, whose electrical research had confirmed Franklin's discoveries. Other club members included James Burgh, a political writer who taught at a dissenting academy; John Densham, who left the ministry for the mercantile trade; Andrew Kippis, a dissenting minister and unrelenting biographer; Richard Price, philosopher, demographer and political radical; Joseph Priestley, theologian and scientist; and Abraham Rees, encyclopaedist.

James Boswell, who occasionally attended, captured the club in his journal: 'Conversation goes on pretty formally, sometimes sensibly, and sometimes furiously. At nine there is a side-board with Welch rabbits and apple-puffs, porter and beer.' Josiah Quincy Jr clarified what Boswell meant by formal conversation. A Boston patriot who attended the club while visiting London, Quincy recorded one evening's conversation: 'A question was debated by assignment whether capital punishments are in every case warrantable.' Much like the Junto, the Thursday club planned its conversation topics in advance. The pre-planning did not prevent heated conversation, as Boswell suggests, but it did give their discussions some structure.[13]

Not all their conversation was formal, of course. Rees, who called Franklin 'the life of the club', remembered discussing the Royal Society's latest research. Franklin's air bath was another topic that entered the conversation. He boasted that every morning he would rise and pass half an hour in the nude reading or writing. Sometimes he would return to bed afterwards and add another hour or two of sweet, restful sleep.[14]

Densham's mercantile career took him to Portugal, but he missed his clubmates: 'You are a knot of wicked rogues you Cantons, Prices, Burghs and some more of you for letting a body be so long an exile . . . without writing a word to let one know whether alive or dead, and all that.' Densham sent a special treat – a case of Portuguese plums – and named members who deserved them and why: Burgh 'for the long grave phys he puts on when catechising me' and Franklin 'for the good sense he genteely treats us with at the club'.[15]

When the conflict between Britain and America escalated, Franklin's Whiggish club members sympathized with him. Their knowledge of American affairs was exceptional. By and large, the British public knew little about the subject. Franklin embarked on a publicity campaign, contributing numerous articles to the London press, starting with 'A Defense of the Americans', a rousing celebration of the American character. This essay refuted two previous articles in the *London Chronicle* that had impugned the courage and intellect of the colonists. Franklin informed readers that America enjoyed widespread literacy and refuted the cliché about the cultural lag between the Old World and the New. The latest London publications reached the colonies in a matter of weeks, not years.

One of the earlier *Chronicle* contributors was an army officer who championed the bravery and professionalism of British soldiers over provincial troops. Franklin cited numerous examples of colonial soldiers who had acquitted themselves with skill and bravery and, conversely, of cowardly British soldiers. During the Battle of the Monongahela, the Indians had thrown Braddock's redcoats into a panic. In their confusion, the British regulars had shot one another and fled a much smaller force, hastily abandoning their guns and ammunition.[16]

Franklin often used humour to take the edge off his pro-American propaganda. 'The Grand Leap of the Whale' combines folklore and book culture. He borrowed a hyperbole from *Gargantua and Pantagruel*, transplanted it to American soil and thus aligned it with the tall talk that was emerging as an integral part of the American oral tradition. Franklin boasted, 'The very tails of the American sheep are so laden with wool, that each has a car or waggon on four little wheels to support and keep it from trailing on the ground.' His tall talk spoofs British gullibility towards America. Elsewhere the article describes one of nature's grandest spectacles: the sight of whales leaping up Niagara Falls![17]

In the second week of August 1759, Benjamin, William and Peter left London on holiday. (King had run away by this time.) The road to Liverpool took the three through Northwich, where they stopped to tour a salt mine. Franklin's surviving correspondence does not detail the episode, but Defoe made a similar visit, so his account can help reconstruct Franklin's descent to the underworld.

To enter the mine, they had to climb inside a 'bucket', a contraption large enough to fit the three of them. Fastened by chains to a rope, the bucket was lowered 150 feet (46 m). The salt cavern's interior provided

> a most pleasant subterraneous prospect, looking like
> a cathedral supported by rows of pillars, its roof of
> crystal, all of the same rock, transparent and glittering
> from the numerous candles of the workmen, labouring
> with their steel pickaxes in digging it away.[18]

The cavern extended for several acres. Before they ascended, William broke off a hunk of salt crystal, a traditional good luck charm.

The salt cavern got Franklin thinking. Others had theorized that rock salt was what made the sea salty, but this theory presupposed that all water was originally fresh. Franklin theorized the opposite: all water was originally salty; fresh water resulted from evaporation and precipitation. The rock salt in the caverns, he argued, came from the sea. The salt cavern also helped him understand Bartram's mountaintop seashell fossils, which indicated that sea water previously covered much of the planet. The receding water left behind salt deposits.[19]

Around the first of September, they reached Edinburgh, staying for two weeks before taking a loop through Scotland, which encompassed Fife, the home of the University of St Andrews. Earlier that year, the university had awarded Franklin an honorary doctorate of law in absentia. The degree prompted 'B. Franklin, Printer' to start calling himself 'Dr Franklin'.

On their return to London, the Franklins stopped in Berwickshire to visit Henry Home, Lord Kames, the Scottish jurist and critic. One night, Franklin presented his 'Parable against Persecution'. Manoeuvring the conversation to the subject of religious intolerance, he called for a Bible, opened it and, having memorized his parable, pretended to read it: a stranger passing Abraham's tent accepted his offer to spend the night. When his guest refused to bless God before eating because he practised an alternate form of worship, Abraham struck the man and shoved him back into the wilderness. God said to Abraham that his inhospitable behaviour displeased him. Abraham entered the wilderness to retrieve the stranger.

Kames was so delighted with Franklin's parable, he asked for a copy. Franklin hesitated, afraid Kames would print it and thus deprive him of the pleasure he got amusing people with it. But Franklin acquiesced and made a copy of it for Kames. Sure enough, his fear came to pass. Kames published the parable and thus denied him the fun of a favourite hoax.

Franklin would take other summer vacations to break up the lengthy time he spent in London. He travelled to Belgium and Holland with his son; toured the Austrian Netherlands and the Dutch Republic with Richard Jackson, an American sympathizer who served as the Pennsylvania Assembly's colonial agent in Franklin's absence; went with Pringle to Germany one year and France the next; and revisited Scotland and toured Ireland with Jackson.

When Franklin returned from his first trip to Scotland in 1759, the Seven Years War was waning. Pamphleteers, journalists and coffee-house blowhards debated possible peace terms. Should Britain keep Canada, or should it keep Guadeloupe, an island in the West Indies it had seized during the war? The answer seems obvious now, but at the time, many British citizens actually preferred the rich sugar colony. Franklin entered the debate in 1760 with *The Interest of Great Britain Considered*. This pamphlet stressed Canada's economic importance. A masterpiece of style and reason, Franklin's pamphlet helped secure the entirety of Canada for the British Empire.

His political mission achieved its greatest success in 1760. The Pennsylvania governor, remarkably, had gone against the proprietors' instructions and passed an act taxing their lands. Thomas and Richard Penn tried to have it disallowed, but Franklin was ready to fight. He hired lawyers to argue the case before the Lords of Trade, who rejected his argument and recommended the Privy Council annul the act. Franklin appealed to the Privy Council. After guaranteeing that proprietary lands would be taxed fairly, he won the case. The Penns did not see this case as precedent-setting; they would continue to oppose taxes on their lands.

Franklin's legal and diplomatic work on the Assembly's behalf did not stop him from pursuing a variety of creative projects. Musical glasses fascinated him. After tuning the glasses by filling them with different amounts of water, the player would wet a finger and rub the rims to make the glasses sing. Franklin enjoyed their otherworldly sound but, ever the efficiency expert, imagined a better way to arrange them.

To create his 'glass armonica' Franklin had special bowls blown in different sizes with a hole in the centre of each. He placed them on a horizontal rod, actuated by a crank attached to a pedal. His careful gradation of bowl size let him create a more accurate scale than water tuning. In addition, the close proximity of the bowl rims would let the player produce chords with greater ease. Two decades later, Francis Hopkinson would try to invent a keyboard for Franklin's armonica. Explaining his effort, Hopkinson sounds like his mentor: 'The door of experimentation is open.'[20] Even without a keyboard, Franklin's armonica attracted leading composers. Mozart would compose *Adagio and Rondo for Glass Armonica, with Flute, Oboe, Viola and Cello*.

Shopping for books was one of Franklin's greatest pleasures in London. Besides regularly visiting bookshops, he also attended book auctions. One held the first week of April 1762 was tinged with sadness: the auction of James Ralph's library. After returning to

Franklin's glass armonica.

London in 1757, Franklin had renewed his friendship with Ralph, who had become a prominent political journalist. Four months earlier, Franklin had visited Chiswick, where Ralph lived with his eighteen-year-old daughter. Afflicted with a grave illness, Ralph died on 24 January 1762. His daughter died five weeks later. The newspapers reported that she was his only daughter. Franklin knew better. Though he did not know the whereabouts of Mrs T's child, Franklin had befriended Ralph's American daughter Mary and arranged for the auction to benefit her family.[21]

Franklin left London for Philadelphia in August 1762 without his son. Presumably, Peter, whose parents lived in Philadelphia, returned with him, but he disappears from history around this time. William Franklin stayed behind to marry Elizabeth Downes, the daughter of a wealthy Barbados planter. He was also commissioned royal governor of New Jersey, apparently with his father's help. John Stuart, 3rd Earl of Bute, Britain's prime minister, had a passion for music and had Franklin help him build a glass armonica. As a favour, Bute secured the governorship for William, who would return to America in February 1763 to assume the position.[22]

Back in Philadelphia on 1 November, Benjamin Franklin caught up with his post office business. He would spend nearly half a year travelling through the colonies inspecting post offices. This Postmaster General even hand-delivered one piece of mail, bringing Bartram a letter from Collinson, who was wondering about some huge fossilized teeth from Big Bone Lick, a salt marsh south of present-day Cincinnati. They came from the American mastodon, but Collinson did not know that yet. He reiterated his request in a follow-up letter, repeating a Native American legend: 'The Indian tradition is that the monstrous buffaloes were all struck dead by lightening at the licking place, but is it likely to think all the race was here collected and was extinguished at one stroke?'[23] Collinson's question reflects the philosophical problem these massive, yet mysterious creatures posed. It was hard to believe that mastodons still roamed North America, but their extinction would mean the great chain of being had snapped once and for all.

Balthasar Friedrich Leizelt, *Vuë de Philadelphie*, *c*. 1770, etching.

As he travelled around colonial America inspecting post offices, Franklin also visited some of the 'Negro schools' that the Bray Associates had established to observe their students. So far, Peter had shaped Franklin's understanding of the African intellect. Franklin's current observations showed him that Peter's willingness to learn was by no means unique. The students Franklin observed greatly impressed him. He wrote to the Bray Associates:

> I was on the whole much pleas'd, and from what I then saw, have conceiv'd a higher opinion of the natural capacities of the black race, than I had ever before entertained. Their apprehension seems as quick, their memory as strong, and their docility in every respect equal to that of white children.[24]

The French and Indian War had effectively ended on 8 September 1760 with the fall of Montreal, but peace would not be official until the Seven Years War formally ended with the Treaty of Paris in 1763. Violence continued to flare up on the Pennsylvania frontier. On 14 December 1763 men from Paxton, a frontier village, massacred six Susquehanna Indians as a reprisal for a recent attack. The Indians whom the 'Paxton Boys' murdered were not those who had perpetrated the attack; they were Christians. Fourteen Susquehanna Indians were subsequently placed in the workhouse in Lancaster for their protection, but the ruthless Paxton Boys stormed the workhouse and slaughtered them. In late January, Franklin denounced the Paxton Boys in *A Narrative of the Late Massacres*.

Before describing the massacre, Franklin's *Narrative* names some victims and provides brief personal descriptions, making the murders more heinous by stressing the victims' humanity. Franklin anticipates modern anti-racist rhetoric, asking, 'If an Indian injures me, does it follow that I may revenge that injury on all Indians?' Answering this question, he presents an impassioned plea for racial tolerance.[25]

Mobs seldom respond to logic. The first week of February, the Paxton Boys marched on Philadelphia determined to kill the Indians there. The governor did nothing to stop them, so Franklin organized the city's defence. He stood up to the rioters, met with their leaders, asked them to present a list of grievances and persuaded them to disperse. Personally confronting the mob, Franklin demonstrated his leadership and, indeed, his bravery.

His leadership also manifested itself in the Assembly. Despite Franklin's work in London, the political animosity between the Assembly and the proprietors escalated. After the Assembly resolved to pursue a royal charter, Franklin wrote *Cool Thoughts on the Present Situation of Our Public Affairs* to explain its advantages and reassure Pennsylvanians that they would not lose the rights that William Penn's original charter guaranteed. Franklin circulated gratis copies of *Cool Thoughts* for maximum impact.

When Norris resigned as speaker of the Assembly in late May, Franklin replaced him. The Assembly adopted his petition to King George III to change the government from a proprietary to a royal government. *Cool Thoughts* had not persuaded Franklin's staunchest political enemies, who believed he wanted a royal colony to make himself governor. They spread ugly rumours – that Franklin had bilked public funds while in England, that he was an Indian lover, that a maidservant was William's mother. The anger culminated in a bitterly contested election that October. Both Franklin and Rhoads lost their seats in the Assembly.

On the plus side, the anti-proprietary party retained its majority and appointed Franklin and Jackson to serve as joint agents in London. Where Franklin was going, he would not need Rhoads, but he had a job for him in Philadelphia: to design and build a new home on a court off Market Street between Third and Fourth Streets. Deborah, again refusing to cross the ocean, would oversee construction. She and the Rhoads family became close. From the hearth to the smokehouse, Deborah was an excellent cook. Having the Rhoadses to tea one day, she outdid herself with great stacks of buckwheat cakes.[26]

By the second week of December, Franklin was back at Craven Street. Margaret and Polly Stevenson were doing well. Temple, now four, had suffered a series of foster mothers, but his grandfather now arranged for him to attend a school in Kensington run by the forward-thinking educator James Elphinston. Temple would return to Craven Street during his school holidays and became Margaret's little darling.

Franklin had been battling the Penns, their governors and the proprietary party for a decade and a half, but he remained steadfast. Writing to Rhoads, he observed, 'The malice of our adversaries I am well acquainted with, but hitherto it has been harmless; all their arrows shot against us, have been like those that Rabelais speaks of which were headed with butter harden'd in the sun.' Franklin misremembered his source. It was not Rabelais, but Samuel Butler, whose poem 'The Elephant in the Moon' mentions darts headed with 'butter only harden'd in the sun'. Regardless, Franklin expressed optimism: 'As long as I have known the world I have observ'd that wrong is always growing more wrong, till there is no bearing it, and that right however oppos'd, comes right at last.'[27]

Though Franklin had come to London to petition the king to change Pennsylvania to a royal government, the Stamp Act took priority. On 2 February 1765 he and other colonial agents met Prime Minister George Grenville to protest the planned stamp duties. Grenville insisted the colonies must partly bear the expense of the French and Indian War. If they objected to the stamp duties, they should devise a more equitable tax. Franklin suggested the British government issue an American paper currency and use the interest charged for borrowing the money to pay Britain. Grenville ignored him.

The Stamp Act passed the House of Commons on 27 February and received the royal assent on 22 March. Scheduled to take effect on 1 November, it would require Americans to pay taxes on all kinds of printed material: almanacs, bills, diplomas, legal documents, newspapers, playing cards. Franklin did everything he could to prevent the Stamp Act – to no avail. As he told Charles Thomson, 'We might as well have hinder'd the suns setting.' Accepting defeat, Franklin advocated forbearance, believing Britain would not oppress the colonies for long. Other Americans were not as patient or complacent. Led by Patrick Henry, the greatest orator in a land of great orators, Virginia's House of Burgesses passed a set of resolves protesting the Stamp Act and denying the British government the right to tax its colonies.[28]

Franklin's complacency towards the administration was misinterpreted as approval, and, on 16 September, a Philadelphia mob threatened his home. Deborah got Sally to safety, but she stayed behind, angry, armed and ready to fight. She was not about to let the mob torch their brand-new home. Rhoads and friends arrived to thwart the mob. Other protests took place throughout the colonies. The royal governors, William Franklin included, were helpless to stop the protesters or enforce the stamp duties.

Parliament had sorely underestimated colonial opposition to the Stamp Act. Inspired by the American resistance, Franklin published numerous articles against the act. In February 1766 the House of Commons debated the issue. Franklin testified on 13 February. His response to the legislators' questions shows that he was informed, serious and dedicated to the cause of American rights. He answered them with reason and precision, force and spirit. His most unnerving answer came when asked whether British troops could enforce the Stamp Act. Franklin could not see how. He replied, 'They will not find a rebellion; they may indeed make one.'[29]

Strongly influenced by Franklin's testimony, Parliament repealed the Stamp Act. The repeal was a victory for all Americans, but their celebrations ignored an act passed directly afterwards. The Declaratory Act gave Parliament the right to enact whatever laws they deemed necessary to control the colonies: a legislative Sword of Damocles.

Throughout the controversy, Franklin had not lost his sense of humour. After the repeal, he wrote 'The Frenchman and the Poker'. This *jeu d'esprit* reports the rumour that Britain would make the Americans pay for the stamped paper they should have used, which reminded Franklin of the fabled Frenchman who would threaten Englishmen crossing the Pont Neuf with a red-hot poker.[30]

'Pray, Monsieur Anglois', the Frenchman said to one potential victim, 'do me the favour to let me have the honour of thrusting this hot iron into your backside.'

'Begone with your iron, or I'll break your head!' the Englishman exclaimed.

'If you do not chuse it, I do not insist upon it,' the Frenchman replied. 'But at least, you will in justice have the goodness to pay me something for the heating of my iron.'

The Stamp Act symbolizes an issue central to the American Revolution: no taxation without representation. In a democratic society, people should only be taxed by their elected representatives. Colonial legislatures like the Pennsylvania Assembly could levy taxes, but Parliament could not, since the colonies did not elect any members to represent them. The solution seemed obvious to many American colonists and British sympathizers: give the colonies seats in Parliament. But Franklin knew Parliament would never allow the colonies sufficient representation to suit their population.

Franklin's petition to change Pennsylvania into a royal government seemed so hopeless that in June 1767 he wrote to the Assembly requesting permission to come home. Instead, it reappointed him joint agent with Jackson. Over the next four years, the assemblies of Georgia, Massachusetts and New Jersey appointed Franklin their agent, as well.

His defence of colonial American rights was not without personal sacrifice: he missed his daughter's wedding. On

23 October 1767 Sally married Richard Bache, a merchant who had recently emigrated from England. Two years later, she gave birth to their first son, Benjamin Franklin Bache. Franklin did not meet his son-in-law until 1771, when he and Jackson stopped in Lancashire on their way home from Scotland. Bache, who was visiting England to see his mother, accompanied Franklin to London.

The Stevenson household provided a surrogate family for Franklin during his London years. On 10 July 1770 Polly married William Hewson, a leading surgeon and anatomist. Franklin gave the bride away. After their wedding, the Hewsons settled in Craven Street. Hewson continued delivering anatomical lectures and making new discoveries about the circulatory system. When Polly gave birth to William, their first child, Franklin became the boy's godfather. Thomas, a second son, soon followed. Sadly, Hewson cut himself while dissecting a corpse, contracted septicaemia and died on 1 May 1774, four months before the birth of their third child, Elizabeth.

During Franklin's time in London, Craven Street became a regular stop for American travellers. When Francis Hopkinson visited in 1766, Franklin treated him with kindness but discouraged his quest for preferment among the Hopkinson family's London connections.[31] Jonathan Williams, Franklin's grand-nephew, came to London in 1770 after attending Harvard. He continued his studies under his great-uncle's tutelage. Franklin could see Williams's potential and made him his private secretary. Thomas Coombe Jr who had come from Philadelphia to receive Holy Orders, stayed at Craven Street and became devoted to Franklin. Benjamin Rush came to Great Britain to study medicine at Edinburgh. When he visited London, Franklin befriended him and sponsored his trip to France to meet its leading physicians and philosophers. Once Rush returned to Philadelphia, he became a professor of medicine at the University of Pennsylvania.

Continuing to defend Americans and American rights, Franklin critiqued the British government in the London press. His two

J. Heath, engraving after a painting by Robert Edge Pine, *Francis Hopkinson*, *c.* 1780.

most renowned pre-Revolutionary articles appeared in September 1773: 'Rules by Which a Great Empire May Be Reduced to a Small One' and 'An Edict by the King of Prussia'. The first presents a set of twenty numbered paragraphs, each relating a different rule. To ruin a great empire, start with its most distant colonies. Deny colonists the same rights as citizens in the Mother Country. Deny them the same commercial privileges, too. And deny them representation in Parliament. Essentially, Franklin's rules tell British administrators to keep doing what they were doing. 'Rules' was widely reprinted, but its satire was lost on Lord North's government, which would enact into law many bills not dissimilar to Franklin's facetious rules.

'An Edict by the King of Prussia' has a frame narrative structure. A contributor from Danzig, a city that symbolized freedom, introduces the edict and thus provides an ironic contrast. Instead of inventing a fictional persona, Franklin wrote as Frederick the Great, a ruler with a reputation for making other lands his own. Frederick's renown contributed to the edict's verisimilitude.

Frederick argues that the earliest British settlements were German colonies, which flourished because of Prussian protection: an argument the British made about their American colonies. Frederick asserts that Britain has yet to compensate Mother Prussia for all it has done. Consequently, Frederick levies a duty on British imports and exports. All ships to and from Britain must touch at Königsberg, where they would be unloaded, searched and assessed the appropriate duties.

Next, Frederick regulates Britain's natural resources, paralleling regulations the British imposed on American colonies. Britain still let Americans mine iron ore and smelt iron but now forbade them from manufacturing ironware. Instead, the colonists had to ship their pig iron to Britain, where it would be manufactured into goods, which were shipped back and sold to the colonists. Frederick follows suit. Britain similarly restricted the manufacture of fur hats and the production of wool. Frederick decrees that the British may trap or trade for pelts but must send them to Prussia to be made into hats. Frederick will let his British subjects raise sheep but prevents them from weaving kerseys or knitting jerseys. If they wish, they could use their wool as manure.

Closing the article after the edict, the Danziger essentially reveals the hoax. He reports the rumour that Frederick had copied his regulations from British parliamentary acts but refuses to believe that Britain, known for its love of liberty, would 'from mean and injudicious views of petty immediate profit, treat its own children in a manner so arbitrary and tyrannical!'[32]

As Massachusetts agent, Franklin learned that Governor Thomas Hutchinson and Lieutenant Governor Andrew Oliver had spearheaded the repressive measures the Crown was taking against the colony. Somehow Franklin obtained their correspondence with Thomas Whately, undersecretary of state, and sent it to Thomas Cushing, speaker of the Massachusetts Assembly. Franklin assumed the correspondence would pacify Massachusetts radicals and allay their ire towards the British authorities. He was wrong. It had the opposite effect, increasing tension between governor and legislature, which petitioned to remove Hutchinson and Oliver from office.

Hutchinson obtained a copy of the letter Franklin had written to Cushing, which urged colonial assemblies to resolve never to aid Britain in any general war unless and until both Parliament and the Crown acknowledged American rights. Hutchinson sent a copy to the colonial secretary, who judged it treasonable and asked General Thomas Gage to obtain Franklin's original letter, so he could be prosecuted. Gage could not locate the original, which had apparently been destroyed.

After Franklin forwarded the Massachusetts petition to remove Hutchinson and Oliver to the British government, a preliminary hearing took place on 11 January 1774. Before any further action, the explosive news about the Boston Tea Party reached London. Furious with Massachusetts, the British sought a scapegoat. The hearing on the petition took place before the Privy Council on 29 January at Whitehall in the Cockpit, a venue originally built for cockfighting.

Franklin shaped his personal appearance as carefully as he crafted his literary personae. Coming before the Privy Council, he wore what one witness called 'a full dress suit of spotted

Unknown artist, *Alexander Wedderburn, 1st Earl of Rosslyn (Lord Loughborough)*, *c*. 1780, engraving.

Manchester velvet', that is, a formal, three-piece suit made from printed cotton velvet, not true silk velvet. Franklin's choice of apparel showed respect for the Privy Council, appreciation of the British textile industry and financial conservatism.[33]

Once Solicitor General Alexander Wedderburn began speaking, it was obvious he had come not to prosecute Franklin but to humiliate him. Wedderburn's grizzle blanketed his head and shoulders but could not mask his smirky black eyebrows. For over an hour, he spewed a torrent of lies, rancour, innuendo and mean-spirited misinformation. Priestley, who had obtained special admission to the Cockpit, saw and heard members of the Privy Council laugh at Wedderburn's sarcastic attacks. He demanded that Franklin be branded a criminal, literally branded. Once the event ended, Wedderburn stepped forward to greet Priestley, whom he knew personally. Priestley snubbed him and left the Cockpit with Franklin.[34]

When news of Franklin's ignominy reached Philadelphia, angry protesters came out on his side. People carried effigies of both Hutchinson and Wedderburn through the streets, ultimately hanging them and burning them. Best of all, they burned the effigies with electricity! The protesters' obvious anger demonstrated that they would willingly perform in reality what they were doing now in effigy.

5

The Declaration of Independence

Two days after facing Wedderburn at the Cockpit, Franklin was
dismissed from his position as Deputy Postmaster General of
North America. No matter: he still had other important work to do.
Instead of catching the next boat to Philadelphia after Wedderburn
humiliated him, Franklin continued to fulfil his responsibilities
as agent for the colonies he represented. Massachusetts required
the most work. To punish the colony for the Boston Tea Party,
Parliament passed four laws that Americans called the Coercive
Acts.

The Boston Port Bill, one of the Coercive Acts, would close
Boston Harbor starting on 1 June 1774, continuing until the city
quelled civil unrest and paid for the tea that had been destroyed.
The Coercive Acts also revoked Massachusetts's royal charter;
limited public gatherings; let troops be billeted anywhere
throughout colonial America; and permitted trials to be removed
to Britain, thus depriving American defendants of the right to
trial by a jury of their peers – a mainstay of modern democracy.
In May General Thomas Gage, commander of the British forces
in North America, reached Boston to assume the Massachusetts
governorship. British troops landed the following month in
numbers sufficient to intimidate the Bostonians.

American leaders clamoured for an intercolonial congress
to debate possible measures to resist the British. In the summer
of 1774, individual colonies began choosing delegates to the

John Singleton Copley, *General Thomas Gage*, *c.* 1768, oil on canvas mounted on masonite.

First Continental Congress, which would bring together many outstanding American leaders. The Virginia delegation included Benjamin Harrison, Patrick Henry, George Washington and Peyton Randolph, who would be elected Congressional President. The Massachusetts delegation included John Adams and his kinsman Samuel Adams, mastermind of the Boston Tea Party.

Gathering in Philadelphia, the delegates befriended one another. Prominent Philadelphians hosted get-togethers for them. The home of Samuel and Elizabeth Powel on Third Street, for instance, attracted many delegates. Witty and well read, Elizabeth took an interest in politics. She sparked political discussions and made them sparkle. Franklin and the Powels would become friends once he returned home. John Adams, who had dinner with them one night, was unused to such luxury: tarts, sweetmeats, floating islands, Parmesan cheese and whipped syllabub.[1]

Despite the conviviality that Philadelphia provided, not all the delegates got along. Though he would emerge as one of Congress's most active delegates, Harrison appalled John Adams. Tall and corpulent, he had an oversized sense of humour to match. Adams vowed to work with him despite his personal dislike, but he considered Harrison the Sir John Falstaff of the Continental Congress.[2]

Thomas Jefferson was not yet a Congressional delegate, but his fellow Virginians brought with them copies of the Williamsburg edition of his *Summary View of the Rights of British America*. Reprinted in Philadelphia, Jefferson's pamphlet shaped the thinking of delegates from other colonies. The Massachusetts delegation brought a parallel document, the Suffolk County Resolves, which declared that they did not need to obey the Coercive Acts and advocated resistance to British troops. Less than two weeks after the First Continental Congress convened on 5 September 1774, it endorsed the Suffolk County Resolves.

Writing to Franklin about the latest developments, Thomas Coombe Jr sent him copies of both Jefferson's *Summary View* and the Suffolk County Resolves. Coombe also let Franklin know how his friends were doing. Rhoads had raised a glass to him and, with a sigh, wished he were home again.[3] Though Coombe does not say so, Rhoads was also serving in the Continental Congress. Elected mayor of Philadelphia that October, Rhoads resigned his

Samuel Powel House, 244 South Third Street, Philadelphia, after 1933.

seat in Congress, thinking it improper to serve in both positions simultaneously.

By the time it adjourned in late October, the First Continental Congress had passed a series of resolutions, which were collected together and printed as *The Association, &c.* This document formed an agreement among Americans not to import or consume materials from Great Britain, nor to export agricultural products to Great Britain. The agreement let Americans protest the actions of Parliament and redress grievances of the American people. It enumerated a series of measures they would take. Number eight, for example, encouraged economy, frugality and industry and promoted the development of local manufacturing. It discouraged such forms of extravagance and dissipation as cockfighting, gaming and horse racing.

Before receiving any official correspondence from Congress, Franklin began two sets of negotiations, one with Fothergill and David Barclay, and the other with Lord Howe. Franklin assured them that he did not have the authority to negotiate, but they encouraged him regardless, thinking he might have secret instructions permitting negotiation. Franklin would remain in London until March 1775. On his way home, he would write 'Journal of Negotiations in London', a minor masterpiece that tells the story of his final efforts to achieve a peaceful and equitable coexistence between Britain and its American colonies.[4]

Four years earlier, Franklin had stayed at the country house of Bishop Jonathan Shipley at Twyford. An American sympathizer, Shipley called North America 'the only great nursery of freemen now left on the face of the earth'.[5] While staying with the bishop and his family, Franklin had written the first part of his autobiography, in which he recalled reading John Bunyan. He appreciated Bunyan more for his prose than his piety. Enjoying how Bunyan integrated dialogue and narrative, Franklin followed suit. He incorporated dialogue in his anecdotes, correspondence and autobiographical writings. The dialogue in 'Journal of Negotiations' brings alive the story of Franklin's last year in London.

A Quaker merchant, David Barclay had yet to shift his professional career to banking. (His bank would form the nucleus of Barclays bank.) A pacifist, Barclay dreaded war between Britain and America. With Fothergill, he sought to mediate between Franklin and Lord North's government. In the first week of December 1774, Barclay and Fothergill had Franklin prepare a list of terms that both Britain and America could accept. Once Franklin had drafted 'Hints or Terms for a Durable Union', the three men discussed its individual items. The fifth item, for instance, stipulates that Parliament repeal all acts restraining manufactures in the colonies. Aware the British government felt strongly about restricting colonial manufacture, Barclay and Fothergill urged him to strike this item. Franklin refused, insisting that all citizens of the British Empire had the right to make the most of their natural resources.

The negotiations with Lord Howe took place at his sister's home. To allay suspicion, Caroline Howe invited Franklin to play chess. Not until Christmas day – that is, not until after the two had become avid chess opponents – did Caroline introduce him to her brother, who initiated their negotiations and reassured Franklin of his confidence that together they could reach a solution.

The day after Christmas, Franklin met his most prestigious ally, William Pitt, 1st Earl of Chatham, at Hayes, his elegant country estate. By this time, Franklin had heard from the Continental Congress and received their petition. Howe doubted the petition's viability, predicting its terms would be scattered like the leaves of the Cimmerian Sibyl.[6] Chatham was more hopeful. Franklin indirectly recorded Chatham's response to the actions of the Congressional delegates: 'They had acted, he said with so much temper, moderation and wisdom, that he thought it the most honourable assembly of statesmen since those of the ancient Greeks and Romans in the most virtuous times.'

When they met again, Howe had a copy of 'Hints or Terms for a Durable Union', which surprised Franklin since Barclay and Fothergill had assured him they would keep the document secret. The situation recalls a memorable Poor Richardism: 'Three may keep a secret, if two of them are dead.' Fothergill and Barclay had shared 'Hints' with Howe. What Franklin had considered two sets of negotiations were not really separate. Howe found 'Hints' unacceptable. He wanted to work together with Franklin to reach terms Britain and America could both accept. If Franklin would do so, Howe promised to reward him with a position of his choice. Howe's bribe revealed that he did not understand the mindset of the American patriots. Franklin wrote,

> He expatiated on the infinite service it would be to the nation, and the great merit of being instrumental in so good a work; that he should not think of influencing me by any selfish motive, but certainly I might with reason expect any reward in the power of government to bestow. This to me was what the French call 'spitting in the soup'.

Howe was sincere in his desire to reconcile Britain and America, but his appeal to personal gain was a major error. Neither Franklin nor other Revolutionary American leaders were interested in prestigious positions or hefty sinecures. They wanted their rights restored, the rights everyone in a free, just and democratic society deserved. Franklin's negotiations with Barclay were not dissimilar. Barclay assured Franklin he could have his Postmaster Generalship restored or obtain any other position he wished. Barclay, too, failed to understand what motivated Franklin and his fellow Americans. Franklin could hardly express in strong enough terms 'how improper and disgusting this language was to me'.

The story of Franklin's negotiations culminates on 1 February 1775, the day Chatham presented a speech on the subject to the House of Lords. Considering Chatham's prestige, Franklin was shocked by how the legislators received his bill. He told Charles Thomson that they treated it 'with as much contempt as they could have shown to a ballad offered by a drunken porter'.[7] John Montagu, 4th Earl of Sandwich, who assumed Franklin had written Chatham's proposal, encouraged the House of Lords to reject it and, speaking to his face, called Franklin 'one of the bitterest and most mischievous enemies this country had ever known'.

Understandably, Franklin was fuming when he left the House of Lords. He found it absurd that these narrow-minded legislators claimed 'sovereignty over three millions of virtuous sensible people in America'. Continuing 'Journal of Negotiations', Franklin exclaimed: 'They appear'd to have scarce discretion enough to govern a herd of swine. Hereditary legislators! thought I. There would be more propriety, because less hazard of mischief, in having ([as] in some university of Germany) hereditary professors of mathematicks!'

Seeing little hope of reconciling Britain and America, Franklin longed for home. Some sad news he received from Richard Bache in late February made him all the more anxious to return. Deborah Franklin had suffered a stroke in mid-December. She lingered for a few days, but on 19 December 1774 with neither groan nor sigh, she was, in Bache's words, 'released from a troublesome world, and happily relieved from all future pain and anxiety'. Franklin had not seen his wife in ten years. Now, he would never see her again.[8]

Sunday 19 March was his last day in London. He spent it with Priestley reading the latest American newspapers. Franklin let his friend know what to extract for the London press: an emotionally draining experience. Priestley recalled, 'In reading them, he was frequently not able to proceed for the tears literally running down his cheeks.'[9]

On Monday Franklin and his grandson Temple left London for Portsmouth, where they embarked for America. The six-week passage was quite pleasant. Besides writing 'Journal of Negotiations', Franklin pursued his oceanographic studies. Fascinated with the Gulf Stream and its capacity for making transatlantic travel more efficient, Franklin hoped to study it further. He began taking daily water temperature readings. They varied so little, he abandoned the effort. But when the ship entered a meadow of sargasso on 26 April, the same day Franklin sighted a whale, he resumed his temperature readings. The presence of sargasso and the higher water temperatures, he concluded, indicated the Gulf Stream.

Upon reaching Philadelphia on 5 May, Franklin heard the shocking news from New England. On 19 April eight hundred redcoats had marched on Concord, Massachusetts, where the colonists had a large cache of guns and ammunition. Having been warned by Paul Revere and others, the Massachusetts militia – the Minutemen – were ready. They assembled at Lexington prepared to clash with the British. When the British commander ordered the Americans to disperse, they refused. The redcoats fired upon the Minutemen, killing eight and forcing the remainder to retreat towards Concord.

The Minutemen, one-quarter the size of the British force, established a new position on the farther side of Old North Bridge over the Concord River. This time they successfully resisted the advancing troops and humiliated the British, forcing them to retreat to Boston and harassing them as they went. The Minutemen adapted to the terrain; the redcoats did not. The British army had learned little since the Battle of the Monongahela. Their inability to adjust their fighting techniques to local conditions seemed absurd to Franklin, according to an anecdote Washington enjoyed telling. Franklin learned that the redcoats complained about the ill usage they received from the Minutemen, who got behind stone walls and fired at them. Franklin wondered 'whether there were not two sides to the wall'.[10]

The day after Franklin reached Philadelphia, the Pennsylvania Assembly named him a delegate to the Second Continental Congress, which would convene in Philadelphia on 10 May. Franklin spent early May renewing old friendships and writing to distant friends. He let British correspondents know that Lexington and Concord had effectively united the colonies.

Franklin's correspondents included David Hartley. An MP from Hull, Hartley was also an inventor, having devised a way to fireproof homes. Franklin had witnessed Hartley's fireproofing experiments. The two had become friends and agreed to correspond. Soon after reaching home, Franklin wrote to Hartley: 'I find here all ranks of people in arms, disciplining themselves morning and evening, and am informed that the firmest union prevails throughout North America.' To Shipley, he wrote, 'I met with a most cordial reception, I should say from all parties, but that all parties are now extinguish'd here. Britain has found the means to unite us.'[11]

From London, Franklin had begun corresponding with Pennsylvania botanist Humphry Marshall. Like his cousin John Bartram, Marshall also corresponded with European naturalists and sent them botanical specimens. Marshall wrote to welcome Franklin home. Franklin's reply differs from what he wrote to the MP and the bishop: 'As Britain has begun to use force, it seems absolutely necessary that we should be prepared to repel force by force, which I think, united, we are able to do.' He continued, 'It is a true old saying, that "make yourselves sheep and the wolves will eat you": to which I may add another, "God helps them that help themselves."'[12]

Personal business also required Franklin's attention. That May he reintroduced his son William to his grandson. As royal governor of New Jersey, William Franklin had been upholding British colonial policy since the Stamp Act, which created a rift between father and son. Since William refused to resign his office and join the rebellion, their meeting did not go well. Temple would stay in New Jersey with his father for the summer, but his grandfather insisted he return to Philadelphia in the autumn to begin college.

The First Continental Congress had met at Carpenters' Hall. The Second would meet at the State House, which would become known as Independence Hall once the Declaration of Independence was signed there the following year. The great room's high ceiling gave Independence Hall a sense of grandeur. Touring it in the early twentieth century, Henry James imagined what a Founding Father might have exclaimed upon entering: 'What an admirable place for a Declaration of something! What could one here – what couldn't one really declare?'[13]

With the start of the Second Continental Congress, the greatest American revolutionaries came together for the first time: John Adams, Benjamin Franklin, Thomas Jefferson and George Washington. Peyton Randolph was again elected president but soon left to serve as speaker of the Virginia House of Burgesses. Congress elected John Hancock president to succeed Randolph. Charles Thomson, who had served as secretary to the First Continental Congress, was re-elected to that position. He would remain its secretary as long as the Continental Congress lasted. On Wednesday 14 June Congress voted to form an army. Adams nominated Washington its commander, and on Thursday Congress unanimously approved the nomination. The following week, Washington left Philadelphia for Cambridge, Massachusetts, where he would form the Continental Army and oversee the siege of Boston.

The Continental Congress was not the only legislative body that demanded Franklin's time. He was also a member of the Pennsylvania Assembly. When the Assembly adjourned on 1 June, it appointed a committee of safety to defend Pennsylvania during its recess. As committee president, Franklin ordered construction of *chevaux de frise* – that is, giant wood-and-iron obstructions that could be placed in the river to prevent British war vessels from sailing within range of Philadelphia. The committee also ordered the construction of armed and oar-powered boats 50 feet (15 m) long. Under Franklin's leadership, Pennsylvania did everything possible to defend itself against the formidable British war machine.[14]

The oldest member of the Continental Congress, Franklin was nonetheless its most radical leader. In July he drafted 'Proposed

Articles of Confederation', which asserted America's sovereignty and gave the central government broad powers to unify the colonies. Congress was unwilling to go as far as Franklin proposed. John Adams, one Congressional delegate who was willing to go that far, admired Franklin's brash self-assurance. On 23 July, two days after Franklin introduced 'Proposed Articles of Confederation', Adams described him to his wife Abigail: 'He does not hesitate at our boldest measures, but rather seems to think us, too irresolute, and backward.' Adams then repeated something Franklin had said to him: 'Even if we should be driven to the disagreeable necessity of assuming a total independency, and set up a separate state, we could maintain it.'[15]

In May Congress had appointed Franklin to chair a committee for establishing a postal system. He submitted the committee's report on 25 July. The next day Congress elected him Postmaster General. He served on other committees with diverse purposes: to regulate commerce; to arrange for printing paper currency; to locate supplies of saltpetre, an essential ingredient of gunpowder; to negotiate with Indians; and to consider the conciliatory proposal Lord North had tendered the colonies. The Continental Congress did not adjourn until 1 August.

Once Congress reconvened in September, Franklin, Harrison and Thomas Lynch, a delegate from South Carolina, were appointed to a committee to confer with George Washington at his headquarters. They left Philadelphia on 4 October and reached Cambridge, Massachusetts, on 15 October. The efficiency Washington demonstrated in assembling the Continental Army was impressive. Franklin wrote to Bache, 'Here is a fine healthy army, wanting nothing but some improvement in its officers, which [it] is daily making.' The redcoats had forced some Bostonians from their homes and burned others out of theirs, but local residents remained resolute:

Gilbert Stuart, *John Adams*, *c.* 1800/1815, oil on canvas.

There are as many chearful countenances among those who are driven from house and home at Boston or lost their all at Charlestown, as among other people. Not a murmur has yet been heard, that if they had been less zealous in the cause of liberty they might still have enjoy'd their possessions.[16]

Before leaving Massachusetts, Franklin dined with Abigail Adams. She found him sociable, but not too talkative. Proud of her ability to read people's faces, Abigail thought she could read Franklin like a book, but physiognomy is an inexact science. An English acquaintance had seen a 'Cassius-like sternness' in Franklin's face; Abigail Adams saw kind-hearted benevolence. A preacher's daughter, she read too much religion into Franklin's countenance, but otherwise she could see 'the virtues of his heart, among which patriotism shined in its full lustre'.[17]

Benjamin Blyth, *Abigail Adams*, 1766, pastel on paper.

After Franklin returned to Philadelphia in the second week of November, Congress placed him on a secret committee to establish a network of international correspondents who could aid America in its defence. France had already sent a secret agent, Achard de Bonvouloir, to Philadelphia. He and Franklin held a series of clandestine meetings under the cloak of darkness. Bonvouloir had no written instructions, only verbal ones. France, he intimated, would willingly help America in its resistance to Britain.[18]

Despite his busy committee work, Franklin found time to write some anti-British propaganda. Indulging his love of hoaxes, he wrote 'Bradshaw's Epitaph', pretending it had been written during the previous century to honour the regicide John Bradshaw. The fake epitaph ends with a valid admonition: 'Never forget that rebellion to tyrants is obedience to God.'[19] Jefferson liked Franklin's words so well that he made them his personal motto.

'The Rattlesnake as a Symbol of America', a newspaper essay Franklin wrote that winter, took its inspiration from a militia company emblem: a coiled rattlesnake with the motto 'Don't Tread on Me.' The rattlesnake symbolizes vigilance, but it means much more. Using the feminine pronoun for the rattlesnake, Franklin observes, 'She never begins an attack, nor, when once engaged, ever surrenders: she is therefore an emblem of magnanimity and true courage.' The snake's rattle is an appropriate symbol, as well: 'One of these rattles singly, is incapable of producing sound, but the ringing of thirteen together, is sufficient to alarm the boldest man living.'[20]

Franklin did not write the most influential work of American literature to emerge during the winter of 1775–6, but he helped make it possible. In 1774 Thomas Paine had reached America with little more than a letter of recommendation from Franklin. He became editor of the *Pennsylvania Magazine*, which gave him the journalistic experience leading to his earth-shattering work. *Common Sense* appeared anonymously in the second week

James Watson, after Charles Willson Peale, *Thomas Paine*, 1783, mezzotint on paper.

of January 1776. More clearly and more forcefully than any previous commentator, Paine made the argument for American independence: 'Everything that is right or natural pleads for separation. The blood of the slain, the weeping voice of Nature cries, "'Tis time to part".'[21]

Congress was still not ready to declare independence. Canada remained one unsettled issue. Would it join the American cause? Congress appointed Franklin as a commissioner to Canada. The late winter journey from Philadelphia to Montreal would be arduous,

Mather Brown, *Thomas Jefferson*, 1786, oil on canvas.

but he accepted the appointment. He and his fellow commissioners left Philadelphia on 26 March. Now seventy, Franklin suffered from swollen legs and suppurated boils during the trip but returned from Canada with little gain for his pains. The commissioners failed to convince Canada to join the American cause.

The Canadians were not the only ones who refused to join the Revolution. In January 1776 the New Jersey Militia, acting on a resolution of Congress, had deprived William Franklin of his official functions as royal governor of New Jersey. He was put under house arrest at Perth Amboy until June, when he was sent under armed guard to Connecticut, where he was imprisoned. Broken-hearted by his son's behaviour, Benjamin Franklin refused to intercede.

In June Congress selected a committee to draft the Declaration of Independence: Thomas Jefferson, John Adams, Benjamin Franklin, Robert Livingston and Roger Sherman. As the first name listed, Jefferson chaired the Committee of Five and therefore determined how it would proceed. He chose to write the Declaration of Independence himself and then submit his draft to the committee for its input.

The second paragraph of the Declaration of Independence contains the most eloquent articulation of the idea of natural rights ever written. Nearly 250 years later, it can still raise goosebumps:

> We hold these truths to be self-evident, that all men
> are created equal, that they are endowed by their
> creator with certain unalienable rights, that among
> these are life, liberty and the pursuit of happiness.

Jefferson's initial version of this sentence differs considerably. He and his committee worked hard to get the sentence just right. In the first draft, its initial clause reads, 'We hold these truths to be sacred and undeniable'. Besides contributing to the paragraph's deliberate pace, the conjoined word pair 'sacred and undeniable' suggests that the ensuing truths were sanctioned by God. Out of character for Jefferson, the use of the word 'sacred' may have been a sop for devout delegates. Actually, the word adds ambiguity to the sentence; 'sacred' also has a secular connotation: elsewhere Jefferson used the word to mean unalterable.[22]

Ultimately, Jefferson cancelled 'sacred and undeniable' in favour of 'self-evident'. Franklin, who found the word 'sacred' inappropriate, apparently suggested the change. He, too, recognized the word's secular connotation, having used it that way himself. Reading a British pamphleteer's suggestion that colonial charters did not matter, Franklin wrote, 'The charters are sacred. Violate them, and then the present bond of union (the kingly power over us) will be broken.'[23] Perhaps Franklin disliked Jefferson's deliberate ambiguity. Regardless, 'sacred and undeniable' was out; 'self-evident' was in.

The Declaration of Independence also presents a list of Parliamentary acts that contradicted laws passed by colonial legislatures. Each act is structured as a clause beginning with the preposition 'for'. One item in the list refers primarily to the Massachusetts Government Act of 1774, which changed Massachusetts's long-standing royal charter, making the Crown the sole authority to appoint members of the provincial council and prohibiting town meetings from conducting business. Jefferson conjoined two gerund phrases to form the clause: 'For taking away our charters, and altering fundamentally the forms of our government'.

Another committee member – Franklin most likely – inserted a third gerund phrase in the middle to make the clause read: 'For taking away our charters, abolishing our most valuable laws, and altering fundamentally the forms of our government'.[24] Franklin's revision – if it is Franklin's revision – echoes Jefferson's previous clause: 'For abolishing the free system of English laws in a neighbouring province'. This clause refers to the Quebec Act, which let Parliament govern Quebec without a representative colonial assembly. The revision implies that what the British government had done to Quebec it could easily do to other colonies.

On Friday 28 June the Committee of Five presented the Declaration of Independence to Congress, which delayed its debate until Monday. Despite the gruelling July heat, debate continued all day Monday and into Tuesday. Hearing his finely crafted prose debated and berated, Jefferson could hardly stand to listen. Seated next to him, Franklin could sense his uneasiness.

To comfort him, Franklin told the story of a hatter named John Thompson. Having completed his apprenticeship, Thompson planned to open his own shop. He created a signboard depicting a hat with the following motto: 'John Thompson, Hatter, Makes and Sells Hats for Ready Money'. Thompson asked friends for advice. One found the words 'hatter' and 'makes hats' redundant. Another said he could omit the verb 'makes' because customers would not care who made the hats provided they were stylish and well made. (Franklin's anecdote antedates the 'name-brand' concept.) A third said the words 'for ready money' were superfluous, since local businesses did not generally sell goods on credit. Thompson shortened his motto to 'John Thompson sells hats', but his crowd of maddening friends remained dissatisfied. Another said he could omit 'sells' because no one would expect him to give them away. He could also omit the word 'hats' because the sign depicted a hat. Once they finished their critique, Thompson had reduced his sign to a picture of a hat with his name subjoined.[25]

The revisions that the Declaration of Independence underwent in Congress were not so severe. On Thursday, the Fourth of July, Congress approved the Declaration of Independence with its final changes and ordered it printed. Copies were sent to General Washington, who had relocated the Continental Army to New York after successfully retaking Boston. Washington arranged for the Declaration to be read aloud to all his troops.

The Declaration of Independence would not actually be signed until 2 August. By then, Pennsylvania had elected a new slate of Congressional delegates, which included Benjamin Rush, whose reminiscence captures the moment he and his fellow delegates affixed their names to the official copy.[26] As President

Charles E. Mills, *Benjamin Franklin Signing the Declaration of Independence*, c. 1911, photomechanical print after a painting.

of the Continental Congress, John Hancock signed first. His bold autograph has become a proverbial synonym for a signature. The delegates who signed the Declaration of Independence have become known simply as the 'signers'.

Rush recalled the weighty silence as one delegate after another approached Hancock's table to sign what many considered their own death warrants. According to Rush, it was Harrison, not Franklin, who broke the silence with a dark joke about being hung for high treason. 'I shall have a great advantage over you Mr Gerry when we are all hung for what we are now doing,' Harrison said to Elbridge Gerry, the slender delegate from Massachusetts: 'From the size and weight of my body I shall die in a few minutes, but from the lightness of your body you will dance in the air an hour or two before you are dead.'

As busy as Franklin was in the Continental Congress, he had other simultaneous legislative responsibilities. On 8 July he was elected to the Pennsylvania state convention and, on 16 July, chosen its president. The convention had the responsibility to draft the state constitution. Similar conventions were taking place in other states. Whereas most state constitutions created a governor and a bicameral legislature, Pennsylvania followed Franklin's preference for an executive council instead of a governor and a unicameral legislature, creating a more purely democratic form of government.[27]

In March 1776 Barclay made one further effort towards reconciliation between America and Britain. He and Fothergill still hoped for peace and offered to do whatever they could. Barclay also told Franklin that Lord Howe, who had been selected as a peace commissioner, still hoped to work with him. Howe might more accurately be called a war-and-peace commissioner. With its Prohibitory Act, Parliament established a two-stage pacification: quash the rebellion and then grant pardons to selected rebels.

As an admiral, Lord Howe would command British naval forces, and his younger brother, General William Howe, would replace Gage to command the British Army. Lord Howe reached Halifax, Nova Scotia, in June. Bad weather equals bad timing: storms prevented Howe from reaching New York until the week after Congress declared independence. Howe addressed his official documents to Franklin and sent them ashore under a flag of truce.

Upon receiving them, Washington forwarded Howe's documents to Philadelphia, where they were opened. With Congress's authorization, Franklin wrote to Howe:

> Directing pardons to be offered the colonies, who are the very parties injured, expresses indeed that opinion of our ignorance, baseness, and insensibility which your uninform'd and proud nation has long been pleased to entertain of us; but it can have no other effect than that of increasing our resentment.[28]

Franklin's letter went to General Washington first, who sent it to Howe under a flag of truce on 30 July. Colonel William Palfrey, who was with the party delivering the letter, recorded Howe's reaction: 'I watched his countenance, and observed him often to express marks of surprise. When he had finished reading it, he said his old friend had expressed himself very warmly.'[29]

General William Howe began landing troops on Long Island on 22 August. With 32,000 men, it was the largest expeditionary force

Charles Corbutt (Richard Purcell pseud.), *The Right Hon.ble Richard Lord Howe, Commander in Chief of his Majesty's Fleets in America*, 1777, mezzotint.

in British history. On 27 August the British defeated the Americans in the Battle of Long Island. Three days later, Washington withdrew his army from Brooklyn Heights to Manhattan.

Before letting his brother pursue Washington to Manhattan, Lord Howe made one final attempt at diplomacy. Treating directly with Congress would acknowledge its legitimacy, something he could not do. Instead, Howe asked to see a few members as private individuals. Congress appointed Benjamin Franklin, John Adams and Edward Rutledge to a committee to confer with Lord Howe on Staten Island.

The first night, they reached New Brunswick, New Jersey. The war had already displaced many people, so the three Congressional delegates had trouble finding accommodation. Franklin and Adams had to share a tiny room with one bed and one window. Adams told the story in his autobiography: another memorable episode in American literature about the humorous situations that arise when travellers must share a bed. Like Franklin and Rush, Adams enjoyed using dialogue in his personal anecdotes.[30]

'Oh!' Franklin exclaimed, as Adams shut the window to protect them from the cold. 'Dont shut the window. We shall be suffocated.' Adams said that he feared the cold night air, but Franklin corrected him: 'The air within this chamber will soon be, and indeed is now worse than that without doors.'

Franklin told Adams to open the window and come to bed; he would relate his theory of colds. People do not catch colds from getting cold, Franklin explained. After the long day on the road, his voice was like a lullaby. Adams fell asleep before he could follow the argument. Another time, Franklin gave Rush the short version: 'People often catch cold from one another when shut up together in small close rooms, coaches, etc. And when sitting near and conversing so as to breathe in each others transpiration.'[31] Viruses would not be discovered until the twentieth century, but Franklin understood how they worked. Benjamin Franklin foresaw social distancing.

They met Lord Howe on 11 September. Adams's autobiography provides the best account of the meeting. Military guards had been living in the house where they met, and the place was a mess. To mask the filth, Howe had spread moss and other greenery on the floor to make it, in Adams's eyes, 'not only wholesome but romantically elegant'. Furthermore, Howe entertained them with cold ham, mutton, tongue, good bread and good claret.[32]

As they spoke, Howe said 'that such was his gratitude and affection to this country, on that account, that he felt for America as for a brother, and if America should fall, he should feel and lament it, like the loss of a brother'. Saying he would be mortified if America fell, Howe was trying to sound sympathetic, but implicit within his words was his certainty that the Continental Army would indeed fall in the face of British military superiority. Franklin caught Howe's tone and offered a reply his lordship was not expecting. He implied that Lord Howe should not be so sure that America would fall.

'I hope', said Franklin, 'your lordship will be saved that mortification. America is able to take care of herself.'[33]

With the failure of these talks, Lord Howe let his brother resume the military campaign. On 15 September General Howe began landing troops on Manhattan. The British pushed Washington's army north, first to Harlem Heights and then to White Plains. On 28 October, the British attacked White Plains, driving the Continental soldiers even further north. Washington was running out of room.

Franklin was not around to hear the news from White Plains. After he returned to Philadelphia from Staten Island, Congress appointed him to a three-man commission to visit Paris and negotiate a treaty with France, the first delegation appointed to represent the United States abroad. The two other commissioners, Silas Deane and Arthur Lee, were already in Europe. Deane was in France, seeking to purchase munitions and other goods for America; Lee was in London, acting as confidential agent for Congress's Committee of Secret Correspondence. On 27 October, the day before the British attacked White Plains, Franklin, accompanied by two grandsons – Temple Franklin, now sixteen, and Benny Bache, who was seven – boarded the *Reprisal*, bound for France.

6

An American Diplomat in Paris

Soon after reaching Paris, Franklin offered some English friends a vivid pen portrait of himself. Though he had worn a peruke to carry out his political and diplomatic work in London, Franklin would wear one no longer. In Paris, he dressed plainly and wore his own thin, grey, straight hair, which poked out from under a fur cap made from the marten *Martes americana*. His cap came down his forehead and almost touched the top of his ever-present spectacles.[1] More posh than Davy Crockett's coonskin cap, Franklin's marten fur cap was no less American. Forbidden from manufacturing fur hats from locally trapped pelts before the Revolutionary War began, Americans could now make hats.

Given his distinctive appearance, scientific accomplishments and winning personality, Franklin became the darling of Paris. Borrowing a comparison from motion pictures, Theodore Hornberger said the French gave Franklin 'the adulation usually reserved for matinee idols'. Though on the right track, Hornberger's comparison is imprecise. Instead of a matinee heartthrob, Franklin more closely resembles a *génie provocateur*, Orson Welles. Like Franklin, Welles achieved larger-than-life status in France during his own time. It is not coincidental that French directors cast Welles as Franklin in two different feature films.[2]

Portraits of Franklin proliferated in France. Parisians hung engraved images of him in their homes, and medallions made from Sèvres porcelain depicting Franklin in profile became chic accessories. His face appeared on clocks, handkerchiefs, rings and snuff-boxes. So many French children had Franklin dolls that he told his daughter Sally that Paris 'i-doll-ized' him. King Louis XVI grew jealous of Franklin's popularity. When a countess joined the throng of idolaters, the king, according to one traditional story, gave her a chamber pot he had custom-made at Sèvres. Inside, Franklin's face adorned its bottom.[3]

Franklin had reached Paris with his grandsons in the first week of December 1776. Before the month had ended, he secretly met Charles Gravier, comte de Vergennes, the French foreign minister. Together they laid the groundwork for diplomatic relations between France and the United States. Franklin found in Vergennes sympathy mixed with shrewdness. His profound dislike of Britain made Vergennes amenable to the American cause, but he would not commit France fully unless and until he could be reasonably sure of victory.

Besides meeting the other members of the commission – Silas Deane and Arthur Lee – Franklin got reacquainted with some men he had known in England. His grand-nephew Jonathan Williams, who was serving as an American naval agent at Nantes, often came to Paris to see him. Edward Bancroft, a Boston-born author and scientist who had studied under Deane and whom Franklin had befriended in London, now served as Deane's secretary. Once Franklin had arrived, Bancroft became secretary for the American legation. He also spied on the British during frequent trips to London.

The British spies in Paris considered Bancroft a possible asset and sought to turn him, which proved surprisingly easy. They simply offered Bancroft more money than the Americans paid. He became a double agent, collecting a spy salary from each side. A quick study, Bancroft developed an in-depth knowledge of espionage tradecraft. He would write secret messages in invisible ink in the margins of love letters and use a dead drop – a sealed

John A. O'Neill, after Charles Nicholas Cochin, *Benjamin Franklin and His Hat, 1777*, 1856, engraving.

bottle in a hole in a tree on the south terrace of the Tuileries – to get his message to his handler. Bancroft would serve as a British spy for years without the Americans catching on.[4]

The American commissioners had the task of negotiating military and commercial treaties between France and the United States. They also sought financial assistance from France. On 5 January 1777 they formally requested French aid. Within two weeks, they had received a verbal promise of 2 million livres. Throughout the

Revolutionary War, Franklin would successfully negotiate further loans from the French government, which could hardly afford what the Americans asked. That Franklin continued to secure loans from France is a testament to his ability to parlay his personal charm into diplomatic currency. The treaties proved more difficult.

In late February 1777 Franklin moved to Passy, then a Paris suburb. He settled into the Hôtel de Valentinois, which became the headquarters of the American legation. Like the neighbouring villas, this one stood on the crest of a bluff. Terraces and gardens led from the villa down to the Seine, which Franklin described in a self-parody, 'Dialogue between the Gout and Mr Franklin'. Suffering from the gout during his Paris years, he personified his disease and, in so doing, made it a worthy Socratic opponent. Gout castigates Franklin for not getting off his duff, for enjoying the view of the exquisite gardens below without descending to them for some much-needed exercise.[5]

'Dialogue between the Gout and Mr Franklin' is one of many bagatelles he wrote at Passy. Before Franklin came along, the word 'bagatelle' did not have a literary connotation. Abel Boyer, the author of the French–English dictionary that Franklin owned, called a bagatelle 'a trifle, a toy, an idle thing, a thing of small value'.[6] Franklin made the word a literary term to describe the playful compositions he wrote at Passy.

Whereas form defines most literary genres, tone defines the bagatelle. Its form can range from parodic dialogue to mock scripture to satirical rhetoric, but its tone is light and bouncy. Contexts of reading also help define the genre. Bagatelles are not intended for publication. Instead, they are designed to circulate privately in manuscript within small, select groups of readers. Sometimes they are so amusing their readers publish them without their authors' consent.

The first bagatelle Franklin wrote at Passy is 'The Sale of the Hessians'. Even as he defined the genre, Franklin expanded its range. Though humorous, 'The Sale of the Hessians' is quite dark. It concerns the death of soldiers belonging to a mercenary force from Hesse, which the British had enlisted to aid them in the American war. Franklin wrote it in late February or early March 1777 – that is, soon after news of the Battle of Trenton reached Paris: the first good news he had received from America.

On 16 November the British had captured Fort Washington, the last American outpost on Manhattan, taking nearly 3,000 soldiers prisoner. From Fort Washington, the British crossed the Hudson River to pursue the severely depleted Continental Army. In the second week of December, General Washington crossed the Delaware River from New Jersey into Pennsylvania. With winter approaching, General Howe paused his military campaign until the following year. He settled his army in winter quarters, dispersing his troops into garrisons throughout New Jersey. The Hessians were garrisoned in Trenton. On Christmas night, Washington famously led 2,400 troops across the Delaware. They attacked the Hessian garrison at Trenton on the morning of 26 December, taking nine hundred prisoners.

'The Sale of the Hessians' is a mock letter from the Count de Schaumburg – the *nom de guerre* of the Landgrave of Hesse – to the Baron of Hohendorf, the commander of Hessian troops in America. Schaumburg congratulates Hohendorf on his heavy casualties – 1,605 men killed, Franklin exaggerated – and reminds his commander that the British were paying him on a per capita basis: the more of his own soldiers killed in action, the better. Don't worry about running out of men, Schaumburg reassures his commander. We can always send boys. Schaumburg hopes the Hessian casualties will increase because he needs the money to pay for his Italian holiday. Depicting soldiers as commodities that can be converted into cash upon their death, 'The Sale of the Hessians' lampoons leaders with neither heart nor soul nor conscience, who line their own pockets by gambling away the lives of those they are sworn to protect.

Given that a small, intimate audience is a defining feature of the bagatelle, Franklin found himself surrounded by an ideal readership at Passy. He established overlapping circles of French friends, including several attractive women. Over a half century ago, Claude-Anne Lopez challenged the myth that Franklin behaved like an old lecher in Paris. Her study, *Mon Cher Papa: Franklin and the Ladies of Paris,* constitutes a three-hundred-page refutation. Regardless, the myth endures, especially in popular culture. Identifying Franklin's penchant for magic squares, Steve Martin conjectures, 'I assume he tackled them when he was not preoccupied with boffing a Parisian beauty.'[7]

Franklin may not have been an old lecher, but he was quite a flirt. Three Parisian women captured his attention more than any others. Anne-Louise Brillon de Jouy, a musician and composer who lived nearby, pleased Franklin even as she teased him. Sophie d'Houdetot had inspired Jean-Jacques Rousseau's best-selling novel *La Nouvelle Héloïse*. Pierre Choderlos de Laclos, the author of *Les Liaisons dangereuses,* said of her, 'She knows that the great affair of life is love.'[8] Anne-Catherine de Ligniville, Madame Helvétius, was the widow of the renowned philosopher Claude-Adrien Helvétius. At her house in Auteuil near the Bois de Boulogne, she hosted a salon that lured some of the best minds in Paris, including the astronomer Joseph-Jérôme de Lalande, the linguist Antoine Court de Gébelin and the historian Constantin-François Volney.

After his success at Trenton, Washington scored another victory a week later at Princeton. The rest of the winter, the Continental Army engaged in a successful *petite guerre* campaign, attacking British troops whenever they ventured out to find forage for their horses. But once General Howe began his 1777 summer campaign, Washington could not stop him from taking Philadelphia. To calm the French, Franklin joked about the fall of Philadelphia, but his jokes fell flat. Vergennes still hesitated to commit French forces to the American cause.

V. De Paredes, *Benjamin Franklin, the United States First Ambassador at the Court of France*, c. 1910, photogravure.

Franklin did not receive any more good news from America until the first week of December, when he learned that the Continental Army had trounced the British at Saratoga. Madame Brillon composed 'Marche des insurgents' to celebrate the victory. The news reignited Franklin's negotiations with the French. On 6 February 1778 the United States and France signed two treaties, a treaty of alliance for mutual defence and a treaty of amity and commerce. In a symbolic gesture, Franklin wore to the signing ceremony the same suit of spotted Manchester velvet he had worn when Wedderburn excoriated him in the Cockpit. Knowledge of these treaties soon reached Great Britain. The British were shocked. Not only were they fighting the rebellious Americans, they now had to fight their long-standing nemesis, an enemy with a powerful army and an intrepid navy. Spain, France's closest ally, would also join the fight. Spain stopped short of recognizing U.S. independence, unwilling to give its own American colonists any ideas.

That the American commissioners had managed to sign the treaties with France was something of a miracle, given their inability to cooperate with one another. Though dedicated to the American cause, Lee's contentious nature got him into trouble. He accused Deane of embezzling congressional funds, which resulted in Deane's recall. Lee also critiqued the way Franklin carried out their commission and became disgruntled with France and other European nations. Lee could not understand why they did not instantly side with the United States. He grew frustrated with Franklin's prudent and more patient diplomatic approach. Franklin understood what Lee could not, that diplomacy takes time, that the nations of Europe had to be courted, persuaded and convinced of the American cause before they would recognize or aid the United States in its war against Great Britain.

Congress appointed John Adams to take Deane's place. Adams did not reach Paris until after the Saratoga news, which effectively accomplished his mission for him. Though Adams had developed a great respect for Franklin when they served together in the Continental Congress, his attitude soured in Paris. Motivated by paranoia and jealousy, Adams imagined that Franklin and Vergennes had ganged up against him. Unable to assail Franklin's lofty position with the French, Adams took out his dislike on Franklin's grand-nephew Jonathan Williams and got him dismissed from his position as naval agent in Nantes.

Two more American officials, Ralph Izard and William Lee – Arthur's brother – made matters worse. Congress had appointed Izard the American commissioner to Tuscany and Lee commissioner to Vienna. Neither Tuscany nor Vienna recognized them, so Izard and Lee stayed in Paris to meddle with the U.S. commission. Taking Arthur Lee's side, they annoyed Franklin at every turn.

Unintentionally, France solved the petty squabbles among the American commissioners. Since France sent a minister plenipotentiary to the United States, protocol demanded that Congress fill a similar position in France. Congress elevated Franklin to the position of minister plenipotentiary, clarifying any ambiguity about who was in charge and rendering the other commissioners superfluous. Franklin fulfilled his diplomatic responsibilities with diligence and perseverance, but the financial matters gave him great pains. As he told Williams, 'I, in all these mercantile matters, am like a man walking in the dark, I stumble often, and frequently get my shins broke.'[9]

Much as Franklin had befriended London's leading scientists during his time as colonial agent, he befriended France's leading intellectuals during his time in Paris, including Voltaire, most importantly. Franklin had been reading Voltaire since the 1730s, but the story of their personal relationship begins in 1778. It is intertwined with the story of Franklin's Masonic activities in Paris. The meetings between Franklin and Voltaire that year, Owen Aldridge observes, have been 'enshrined as popular anecdotes, resembling legendary tales of the gods and heroes of antiquity'.[10]

In February 1778 Franklin and his grandson visited Voltaire. Franklin asked Voltaire for his benediction of his grandson. Since several people witnessed the event, several versions of it survive. Some say Temple was the grandson Franklin brought; others say Benny received the benediction. The eyewitness accounts generally agree that Voltaire delivered a short but sweeping message to Franklin's grandson: 'God and Liberty.'[11]

Temple had another Voltairesque encounter. Franklin thought the Brillons' older daughter would make the best of all possible granddaughters-in-law and tried to play matchmaker. They had named her Cunégonde after the heroine of *Candide*. There is no saying for sure whether Franklin read *Candide*. His known writings do not mention the book, but one of his French correspondents quoted its famous last line – 'but we must cultivate our garden' – apparently assuming Franklin would get the reference.[12] The

Achille Devéria, *Voltaire Blessing Franklin's Grandson, 1778*, 1826, oil on canvas.

Brillon family rejected the union, citing Temple's Protestantism as a convenient excuse.

A few months after meeting Voltaire, Franklin helped induct him into the Lodge of the Nine Sisters. This Masonic lodge was the brainchild of Helvétius, who had longed to create a lodge resembling a learned society that celebrated and encouraged the arts and sciences. Helvétius died before he could see his dream

Robert-Guillaume Dardel, *Allegory in Praise of Voltaire* (*The Apotheosis of Voltaire*), *c.* 1773–83, oil on canvas.

become reality, but Lalande, with Madame Helvétius's help, created the Lodge of the Nine Sisters, which they named for the nine Muses. Lalande became its first Grand Master.[13]

Voltaire was inducted on 7 April 1778. Then in his eighties, he went through an abbreviated induction ceremony. He was blindfolded prior to the ceremony. Franklin, who was in his seventies, took Voltaire by the arm and led him into the lodge chamber. Imagine the bespectacled Franklin leading the blindfolded Voltaire, as the wide-eyed lodge members looked on in awe. Voltaire's examiners asked him several questions, informed him about the secret signs and symbols of freemasonry, and finally proclaimed him a member of both the order and of the Lodge of the Nine Sisters.[14]

Franklin and Voltaire met once more before the month ended. On 29 April the two attended a meeting of the Paris Academy of

Sciences, which had elected Franklin to membership half a dozen years earlier. Adams, who attended the event, left the fullest account of the evening. When other attendees realized that both Franklin and Voltaire were present, they clamoured for them to be introduced. The two came to the stage, bowed and spoke to one another. The audience wanted more. Franklin and Voltaire shook hands, but the crowd remained dissatisfied. The two must kiss one another on the cheek, the French insisted. So they did. The Marquis de Condorcet, who was also in attendance, compared Franklin with Solon, the renowned Greek legislator, and Voltaire with Sophocles, the renowned Greek tragedian. He was not the only one to make the comparison. Adams recorded the French reaction, but his tone reflects his disdain: 'How charming it was! Oh! it was enchanting to see Solon and Sophocles embracing!'[15]

Voltaire died on 30 May 1778. Six months later, the Lodge of the Nine Sisters held a memorial service. On 28 November the auditorium was draped in black and dramatically lit. Eulogies of Voltaire alternated with original music composed by Jean-Philippe Rameau and Christoph Willibald Gluck. Voltaire's niece – a rare female attendee – presented the lodge with the bust of Voltaire sculpted by Jean-Antoine Houdon. In addition, the lodge unveiled a huge painting of Voltaire's apotheosis. On stage for the unveiling, Franklin removed the laurel crown from his own head and placed it beneath the painting.[16]

The efforts of the Lodge of the Nine Sisters to promote the arts and sciences are consistent with Franklin's other intellectual and diplomatic activities in Paris. On 10 March 1779 he issued 'Passport for Captain Cook'. Addressed to the captains and commanders of u.s. warships, the passport informed them that Cook was returning from a great scientific expedition in the South Pacific. If they encountered the British explorer, they should not consider him an enemy, nor should they plunder his ship, which would be filled with collections valuable to science. Instead, the captains and commanders should treat Cook and his men with kindness and civility.

Unbeknownst to Franklin, Cook would not return to England, having been killed in Hawaii. Regardless, the magnanimity of Franklin's 'Passport for Captain Cook' pleased the international scientific community. With this document, Franklin reasserted the importance of the 'Republic of Letters', an informal, but worldwide literary and scientific community that transcended political boundaries. Citizens of the Republic of Letters understood that international strife should not hinder intellectual progress.

With Lalande's departure as Grand Master, the Lodge of the Nine Sisters elected Franklin his successor on 21 May 1779. Under Franklin's leadership, the lodge established the Apollonian Society with Court de Gébelin as its president. An effort to reform higher education, the Apollonian Society sought to disseminate knowledge as widely as possible. It sponsored scientific and literary lectures for the public – women as well as men.

Franklin's relationship with the Lodge of the Nine Sisters and its Apollonian Society shows that he embraced European scientific societies and encouraged their work. He did not support everything the scientific academies did. From its establishment in 1772, the Imperial and Royal Academy of Sciences and Belles Lettres of Brussels could claim few scientific achievements. To encourage the sciences, this academy organized a series of intellectual contests, for which it awarded medals. In late 1779 the academy prepared four questions, including one in the field of mathematics. Given a certain geometric figure, how many smaller figures could it contain? Franklin found the question silly, especially since it had been puffed for its practical value.

To emphasize its absurdity, Franklin wrote 'To the Royal Academy of Brussels', a bagatelle that would out-Rabelais Rabelais. Franklin dismisses the academy's mathematical question and substitutes a problem of his own, which, he claims, had far more practical value. It concerns the digestive system – namely, the social and physiological problems resulting from the gas that indigestion produces. Those who do not control the release of gas offend other people with its fetid smell. But those who try to prevent noxious gases from escaping risk permanent damage to their own bodies. Franklin's prize question challenges competitors to discover a food additive that could fumigate flatulence.

To assure the academy that this chemical project was no chimerical project, Franklin offered some parallel examples. He observed,

> A little quick-lime thrown into a jakes will correct the amazing quantity of fetid air arising from the vast mass of putrid matter contain'd in such places, and render it rather pleasing to the smell . . . Perhaps a glass of limewater drank at dinner, may have the same effect on the air produc'd in and issuing from our bowels?[17]

He facetiously argued that the person who discovered this food additive would accomplish something better than what the world's best scientists had accomplished:

> What comfort can the vortices of Descartes give to a man who has whirlwinds in his bowels! The knowledge of Newton's mutual attraction of the particles of matter, can it afford ease to him who is rack'd by their mutual repulsion, and the cruel distensions it occasions? The pleasure arising to a few philosophers, from seeing, a few times in their life, the threads of light untwisted, and separated by the Newtonian prism into seven colours, can it be compared with the ease and comfort every man living might feel seven times a day, by discharging freely the wind from his bowels?[18]

He continued in this manner for another two hundred words. By the time he finished, he had created a scatological masterpiece. 'To the Academy of Brussels' is the greatest fart joke in American literature.

Franklin printed 'To the Academy of Brussels' on his private press, making just enough copies to share with friends. He had installed the press at Passy to facilitate his diplomatic work, letting him print passports, promissory notes and other official documents. He took great pleasure in returning to his roots. 'Dr Franklin, Minister Plenipotentiary to the Court of France' once more became 'B. Franklin, Printer'.

The Passy press served another purpose. Franklin had sent Benny to a boarding school in Geneva, but he eventually brought him back to Passy to teach him a career-making skill. Benny Bache would become a leading printer in Philadelphia during President Washington's administration. To Washington's chagrin, Benny would edit and print the *Aurora*, the leading opposition newspaper that relentlessly attacked the nation's first president. Like all good leaders, Washington never let the adverse press ruffle his feathers or rankle his spirit.

During his time in Paris, Franklin kept in touch with Washington. His letters have an avuncular quality. They show the elder man consoling and reassuring the younger, no matter that the younger was a great general. Writing to Washington on 5 March 1780, Franklin projected what America would be like after the Revolutionary War, using a Homeric simile to convey the grandeur of the war and the greatness of their cause.[19] The letter shows Franklin's ability to shape his material to suit his audience. For Washington, who looked forward to returning to his farm at the war's end, Franklin applied some uniquely American agricultural imagery:

Like a field of young Indian corn, which long fair weather
and sunshine had enfeebled and discolour'd, and which
in that weak state, by a thunder gust, of violent wind,
hail and rain seem'd to be threaten'd with absolute
destruction; yet the storm being past, it recovers fresh
verdure, shoots up with double vigour, and delights the eye,
not of its owner only, but of every observing traveller.[20]

Franklin's uplifting letter was one of the few positive pieces of
mail Washington received in 1780. In May the British captured
Charleston, South Carolina, taking more than 5,000 prisoners
and, in so doing, handing the Continental Army its worst defeat
of the war. Lord Cornwallis, who took over Britain's southern
campaign, subsequently routed the American troops under the
command of General Horatio Gates at Camden, South Carolina.
Once Washington had appointed General Nathanael Greene to
succeed Gates in the South, the American war effort took a turn for
the better.

In late 1779 John Adams had been appointed to negotiate a
peace treaty and a commercial treaty with Britain, but the British
refused to recognize Adams's condition for negotiation: American
independence. Thwarted in his mission, Adams stayed in Paris. He
pestered the French foreign minister so incessantly that Vergennes
finally refused to deal with Adams, insisting that in all future
dealings he would work solely with Franklin. Adams's presence
became so annoying that Franklin wrote to Congress and requested
his removal. Congress compromised, creating a new peace
commission that included Adams and Franklin and added John Jay
and Henry Laurens. Before peace talks could begin, Adams went
to the Netherlands, where he worked to negotiate a loan from the
Dutch and secure its recognition of American independence.

When Cornwallis surrendered to Washington at Yorktown,
Virginia, on 18 October 1781, he ended British hopes of a decisive

land victory. Franklin engaged in informal peace negotiations with British envoy Richard Oswald from March to June 1782. The formal negotiations would take much longer. Adams returned to Paris to join the other peace commissioners. Jay insisted on British recognition of American independence as a precondition to formal negotiations. The delay gave Britain an advantage in the war at sea and thus weakened the American bargaining position. Not until 30 November 1782 would Oswald and the American commissioners sign the preliminary articles of peace.

On 20 January 1783 Franklin and Adams went to Versailles to accept the British declaration of the cessation of hostilities. With representatives from Great Britain and Spain, they signed the official documents. The formalities dragged on long enough to test Franklin's legendary patience, and he grew homesick. That July, he informed a correspondent, 'The French are an amiable people to live with: They love me, and I love them. Yet I do not feel my self at home, and I wish to die in my own country.'[21] On 3 September 1783 Adams, Franklin and Jay signed the Treaty of Paris on behalf of the United States, with David Hartley signing on Britain's behalf. Not until 12 May 1784 was the formal ratification of the peace treaty with Great Britain official. The very next day, Franklin wrote to Congress and asked to be relieved from his post, so he could return home.

The peace let him reconnect with the British scientific community. Throughout his time in Paris, Franklin had followed the latest scientific developments, balloon ascensions being the most spectacular. He reported the balloon experiments to the Royal Society. The Mongolfier family, which ran a papermaking concern, invented the hot-air balloon, constructing it from cloth-lined paper. Franklin appreciated the invention but thought it should be made with 'fine oil'd silk' instead. Subsequent balloons were.

Whereas the Mongolfier balloon was a hot-air balloon, the invention of a process for generating hydrogen made lighter-than-air balloons possible. On 27 August 1783 at five o'clock in the afternoon, a new balloon, having been filled with hydrogen, lifted from its moorings at Champ de Mars, as thousands of people – 50,000, Franklin estimated – stared at it in awe. Franklin depicted the balloon rising into the heavens:

> A little rain had wet it, so that it shone, and made an agreeable appearance. It diminish'd in apparent magnitude as it rose, till it enter'd the clouds when it seem'd to me scarce bigger than an orange, and soon after became invisible, the clouds concealing it.[22]

Before 1783 had ended, the first manned balloon flights would take place. Franklin witnessed those, too. Besides being an eyewitness, he also left the most memorable observation to emerge from these spectacular balloon flights. They fascinated the public, but sceptics wondered what possible good could come from such seemingly useless experiments. Franklin found their scepticism absurd. In reply he exclaimed, 'What good is a new-born baby?!' His words were widely repeated and reprinted. Simple as it is, Franklin's rhetorical question represents the single greatest defence of pure research ever made.[23] History, of course, has proven him right. Franklin witnessed nothing less than the birth of air travel.

Franklin's scientific expertise also landed him on a royal commission to investigate Franz Anton Mesmer's bizarre medical practice. Mesmer theorized that 'animal magnetism', an imperceptible fluid that supposedly pervaded the cosmos, affected the movement of all the bodies within it, everything from planets to people. Furthermore, he contended that any illness could be cured using magnetic forces to restore the body's internal harmony.

In the late 1770s Mesmer established his practice in Paris. He added many evocative touches to enhance his magnetic therapy: subtle lighting, strategically placed mirrors and even a glass armonica to contribute to the eerie atmosphere. Mesmer seems like

Expérience Aérostatique Faite Versailles le 19 sept. 1783, etching depicting a balloon launched by the Montgolfier brothers ascending from the Palace of Versailles, France, before the royal family, with a sheep, a duck and a rooster as passengers.

a charlatan, but he genuinely believed in animal magnetism. People visited his clinic with all sorts of ailments. The business proved quite lucrative, but Mesmer wanted more than money. He longed for scientific recognition. To that end, he invited Franklin to tour his clinic. Franklin was unimpressed.

In the face of Mesmer's burgeoning popularity, Louis XVI created a commission to look into mesmerism in March 1784. Since women formed a large percentage of Mesmer's clientele, the king was concerned that he was taking advantage of female patients, touching them inappropriately and producing *titillations délicieuses*. Franklin was chosen president of the commission: another indication of the profound respect the French had for his scientific expertise.[24]

The commission released its report in August 1784. Mesmer had refused to cooperate, but Charles-Nicolas Deslon, his leading

French protégé, gave the commissioners full cooperation. After observing numerous supposedly successful cures, they concluded that magnetism had little or no effect on the body. The patients who showed improvement were those with the best imaginations. They imagined that the magnetic therapy worked, and their physical ailments lessened. The patients' imaginations were solely responsible for their improvement. Animal magnetism itself was bogus.

Franklin's writing took other directions during his Paris years. In 1784 he returned to his autobiography and wrote its second part, the part that famously describes his personal scheme for achieving moral perfection. Starting with temperance, he listed the thirteen virtues he hoped to attain and briefly described how to attain them. He wrote them in a notebook ruled with red ink, which he would mark with a black spot everyday he found fault with himself regarding that particular virtue. At the end of each week, he would erase the marks and start afresh.

The notebook Franklin used was an ivory table book – that is, a pocket notebook with leaves made from ivory, which could be easily erased. The image of Franklin inscribing his ivory table book in the autobiography anticipates Captain Ahab inscribing the medallion-shaped tablet that he has built into his ivory leg in *Moby-Dick*. Franklin abandoned his scheme for achieving moral perfection but kept the notebook and used it for general purposes. Pierre Jean Georges Cabanis – Comtesse d'Houdetot's protégé – befriended Franklin, who discussed his life with him at considerable length. Franklin told Cabanis about his scheme for achieving moral perfection and showed him the ivory table book. Cabanis observed,

It provided a sort of chronological story of the soul and the disposition of Franklin: they could be seen developing, getting stronger, shaping up to all the actions which epitomize their perfection as well as the art of living and practicing virtue, learnt in the same way as that of playing an instrument or going on one's first military campaign.[25]

Looking back at his younger self from the distance of half a century, Franklin does not appear embarrassed with or ashamed of his jejune scheme. He seems quite proud of it. His ample girth and the flare-ups of gout he suffered at Passy reminded him that his efforts towards temperance had not worked as well as he had hoped, but he had more than succeeded with other moral virtues – industry, justice, resolution, sincerity, tranquillity.

Franklin received so many enquiries from Europeans interested in emigrating to America that he grew weary of responding to each. Instead he wrote a general statement and printed it at Passy in English and French. *Information to Those Who Would Remove to America* forms a major contribution to a prominent early American literary genre: promotion literature. As a promotional tract, Franklin's *Information* is second only to Captain John Smith's *Description of New England*.

Though the term 'middle class' had yet to be coined, Franklin adumbrates it as he emphasizes the importance of the 'middling sort'. There are not many poor people in America, he says, but neither are there many rich people. Most belong to the middling sort: farmers, artisans, merchants. High birth means nothing to Americans: 'People do not enquire concerning a stranger, "What is he?" but "What can he do?"'

Franklin refutes the stereotype that America is a fantasyland:

In short America is the Land of Labour, and by no means what the English call Lubberland, and the French call Pays de Cocagne, where the streets are said to be pav'd with half-peck loaves, the houses til'd with pancakes, and where the fowls fly about ready roasted, crying, 'Come eat me!'

Since land was cheap and plentiful in America, people who were willing to work hard could get ahead. George Washington left one of the finest appreciations of Franklin's promotional tract: 'Short as it is, it contains almost every thing that needs to be known on the subject of migrating to this country.'[26]

Not until 2 May 1785 did Franklin receive permission from Congress to come home. In Paris since the previous year, Jefferson had been part of a new commission to negotiate treaties of amity and commerce with other European nations. Taking Franklin's place as minister plenipotentiary, Jefferson faced a difficult task. He would do an excellent job but still could not approach his predecessor. Claude-Anne Lopez succinctly characterizes Franklin's place in the history of u.s. diplomacy: he was 'the greatest ambassador that America ever sent to France'.[27] Telling French acquaintances and officials about his new position in the coming weeks, Jefferson had to endure the same question time and again as they asked if he would replace Franklin. 'No one can replace him,' Jefferson would reply. 'I am only his successor.'

7

The Nestor of America

Franklin's numerous inventions include a new kind of spectacles. Precisely when he invented them is uncertain, but his fullest description occurs in a letter he wrote to a London friend from Paris in May 1785. Observing that lenses for seeing distances differed from those for seeing close up, Franklin told his friend he used to carry two pair of spectacles and switch them as necessary, an inconvenience that slowed his reading and limited his enjoyment of the scenery. Consequently, he had a new pair made: 'I had the glasses cut, and half of each kind associated in the same circle . . . By this means, as I wear my spectacles constantly I have only to move my eyes up or down as I want to see distinctly far or near, the proper glasses being always ready.'[1]

He called this new style of eyeglasses his 'double spectacles', but what Franklin had invented was nothing short of bifocals. That term would not be coined until the late nineteenth century, but Franklin deserves credit for creating the first bifocals, his greatest invention since the lightning rod. As with the Franklin stove, the glass armonica and the lightning rod, he did not patent his double spectacles. Since the inventions of others had improved his life, he wanted his inventions to improve the lives of others and refused to profit from them materially.

Franklin would not leave Passy until 12 July. Jefferson, who watched him say goodbye to his French friends, recorded the moment for posterity. He wrote that several women smothered 'mon cher papa' with kisses. Franklin introduced them to Jefferson, his successor, who, referring to their affectionate embraces, wished he would transfer that privilege to him. Franklin replied, 'You are too young a man.'[2]

Still plagued with bladder stones, Franklin found coach travel excruciating, so Queen Marie Antoinette let him use one of her litters. Suspended by two Spanish mules, the litter slowly carried Franklin to Le Havre. Temple and Benny accompanied him. They sailed from Le Havre on Friday 22 July, reaching Southampton, England, on Sunday. William Franklin, now living in England, came to see his father at Southampton. So did Bishop Shipley and other English friends. Jonathan Williams also met Franklin there. He was ready to go home and joined his great uncle for the trip across the Atlantic.

Franklin sailed for Philadelphia on 28 July. As in all his previous ocean crossings, he found much to keep himself busy. While still in Paris, he had started 'Maritime Observations', which he continued aboard ship. He wrote it in the form of a letter to Julien-David Le Roy, who had accomplished much practical research on navigation. Fewer than ten pages into this forty-page work, Franklin says, 'The garrulity of the old man has got hold of me, and, as I may never have another occasion of writing on this subject, I think I may as well now, once for all, empty my nautical budget.'[3]

What stands out most about 'Maritime Observations' is the diversity of Franklin's material, which comes from books, experiments, empirical data, folk wisdom, personal acquaintances and knowledge gleaned from his previous ocean crossings. To test his theories about the size, shape and positioning of different sails, Franklin, while still in Paris, had snipped some vanes from a tin plate, mounted them on his roasting spit in different configurations and passed a current of air over them. Aboard ship, he continued studying the Gulf Stream, measuring changes in temperature and recording weather conditions.

Franklin's design for bifocals, in a letter to George Whatley, 23 May 1785.

In 'Maritime Observations', Franklin mentions 'the well-known practice of the Chinese to divide the hold of a great ship into a number of separate chambers by partitions tight caulked'. Franklin does not name his source, which has so far gone unnoticed, but he was recalling William Dampier's *New Voyage Round the World*, which describes the construction of Chinese junks.[4] Explaining how to design a sea anchor for holding a ship during rough weather, Franklin recalls what he learned from 'an ingenious old mariner'. 'Maritime Observations' also provides some useful advice for travellers. Franklin recommends travelling with a portable

Charles B. J. Févret de Saint-Mémin, *Jonathan Williams*, 1798, engraving.

camp-stove and some staple foodstuffs to avoid the notoriously
poor cooking at sea, which is reflected by a popular sailor saying:
'God sends meat, but the Devil cooks.'[5]

Jonathan Williams's presence aboard ship gave Franklin the
opportunity for much scientific conversation. Williams was
fascinated with Franklin's research into the Gulf Stream and agreed
to help him measure the air and water temperature throughout the
voyage. Williams would continue Franklin's research, eventually
publishing his results as *Thermometrical Navigation*. One need not
go beyond Williams's title page to see his great uncle's influence.
He used a Poor Richardism for its motto: 'God helps them that help

themselves.' His subsequent career reflects Franklin's enduring influence. The first superintendent of West Point, Williams would establish an innovative curriculum and make the military academy the first school of scientific engineering in the United States.[6]

The science of sailing was not the only topic that occupied Franklin on this crossing. He also returned to chimneys. Written in the form of a letter to his friend Jan Ingenhousz, the work would be published as *Observations on the Causes and Cure of Smoky Chimneys*. Reprinted in London two years later, this little treatise elicited a long but hitherto unrecorded review from the *Whitehall Evening-Post*. While appreciating the treatise, the review devotes most of its attention to express surprise. An indication of the profound respect the British had for Franklin, this review deserves lengthy quotation:

> Smoky chimneys! Heaven defend us, what a subject to occupy the pen of his Excellency the great Dr Franklin! After a moment's recollection, however, we cease to wonder that the Doctor should thus employ his talents. Who knows not, as well as we know, that his Excellency is an old, and an experienced smoker – smoker, we mean, of men and things? Who knows not also how admirably the olfactory nerves of this illustrious gentleman were calculated, many years ago, to smell the smoke of British gun-powder long before Britain thought of firing a shot? Nay, who knows not, 'moreover and also', how dextrously, and how patriotically, he afterwards contrived so to regulate and direct the smoke of American gun-powder as to free his beloved country from clouds ever since?[7]

Before reaching Philadelphia, Franklin had the opportunity to discuss the arts as well as the sciences. His fellow passengers included the sculptor Jean-Antoine Houdon. To capitalize on Franklin's huge popularity in France, Houdon had created busts of Franklin in terracotta, marble and plaster. He was now going to

America to sculpt Washington's head as part of the preliminary work for creating a life-sized statue. Many consider Houdon's *Washington* his masterpiece. Installed in the Virginia Capitol in Richmond, it would encourage the development of monumental sculptural art in the United States.[8]

Franklin landed at Philadelphia on 14 September to the sounds of cannon salutes, pealing bells and cheering crowds. Though he had been looking forward to his retirement, he found many demands on his time. For years he had been serving in absentia as president of the American Philosophical Society, but now he took the chair for the first time. It was one of many organizations with which he became active upon his return.

At the October meeting of the Philadelphia Society for Promoting Agriculture, Franklin was proposed for membership. The brainchild of John Beale Bordley – Quirpum Comic – this organization had been founded earlier that year. Since Franklin last saw him, Bordley had inherited Wye Island near the mouth of the Wye River, where he established The Vineyards, a 1,600-acre (650 ha) farm that let him perform numerous agricultural experiments. Samuel Powel, who lived in Philadelphia but had a farm outside of town, had been elected president of this new organization, Bordley vice president. In November 1785 Franklin was elected a member. He was never very active with the agricultural society, but Temple also joined, so he could report its proceedings to his grandfather.[9]

On 11 October Franklin was elected to the Supreme Executive Council of Pennsylvania for a three-year term, and the following week the council and the assembly together elected him president. They would unanimously re-elect him to the presidency for the next two years: the maximum the state constitution allowed. As president of the Supreme Executive Council, Franklin effectively performed the role of the governor of Pennsylvania. The dreams he had entertained of a relaxing retirement disappeared with this new responsibility, but he was proud to serve Pennsylvania.

Humphry Marshall contacted Franklin in early December and sent him a copy of his recently published book, *Arbustrum Americanum: The American Grove*. Marshall dedicated the book to Franklin and the membership of the American Philosophical Society. Besides its appearance in the dedication, Franklin's name occurs later in the volume. Marshall's book represents the first publication of a species of plant that William Bartram had discovered. Bartram named the plant after Franklin: *Franklinia alatamaha*.[10]

Marshall also provided a brief account of its discovery. William Bartram had not become a professional engraver, as Franklin had recommended. Instead, he followed in his father's footsteps and became a botanist, a scientific career that let him apply his artistic abilities. In 1765 John and William Bartram travelled from Charleston, South Carolina, to Florida. Along the Altamaha River in eastern Georgia, they discovered the unknown species, a tree in the tea family. Returning to the region the following decade, William Bartram encountered the species again, this time in full bloom and bearing fruit. He collected seeds and began cultivating it at his Philadelphia nursery. *Franklinia alatamaha* would become extinct in the wild. It survives today solely because William Bartram cultivated it.[11]

Many people visiting Philadelphia in the mid-1780s hoped to meet Franklin. Andrew Ellicott's surveying career fostered his scientific interest in astronomy and mathematics. He and Franklin met the first week of December, and Franklin invited him to spend that Sunday at Franklin Court. Ellicott's diary captures Franklin in a quiet moment. Once he had entered Franklin's house, Ellicott found him in a little room filled with 'old philosophical instruments, papers, boxes, tables, and stools'.[12]

The cramped quarters reveal a problem Franklin faced upon his return. This, the home Rhoads had built for him and Deborah, had filled up with little Baches while Franklin was abroad: Sarah and

Richard now had six children. Franklin faced the daunting task of finding room for his personal library, which had swelled to over 4,000 volumes. He decided to build a large addition to his home. The first floor would be a dining room that could seat 24. The library, 16 × 30½ feet (5 × 9 m), occupied the entire second floor of the new wing.[13]

During construction, Franklin took down a lightning rod he had installed earlier and discovered that 'the copper point which had been nine inches long, and in its thickest part about one third of an inch diameter, had been almost all melted and blown away, very little of it remaining attach'd to the iron rod.' He modestly concluded, 'At length the invention has been of some use to the inventor.'[14]

Franklin devised an innovative cataloguing scheme that let him easily access his books. His scheme is consistent with other clever devices he created in the late 1780s to facilitate the use of his library. He invented a chair that transformed into a stepladder for accessing the topmost shelves, which extended to the ceiling. He also devised a kind of mechanical hand that could gently remove individual volumes from the upper shelves like a sticky-fingered giant. Even with the added convenience of his new inventions, Franklin was not organizing the library himself. Benny and Temple were helping him with the task. They were the ones scrambling up and down their grandfather's ingenious stepladder.

Franklin's library became a frequent meeting place for a new organization he founded, the Society for Political Inquiries. At its first meeting on 9 February 1787, Franklin was elected president. Family members joined: Richard Bache, Temple Franklin and Jonathan Williams. The membership also included other familiar names: Francis Hopkinson, Thomas Paine, Samuel Powel and Benjamin Rush. No doubt Elizabeth Powel would have joined had they let women be members. The organization was part Junto and part American Philosophical Society. Like the Junto and the

Club of Honest Whigs, the new society would assign questions for discussion ahead of time. Much as the American Philosophical Society studied the natural sciences, the new organization would study political science. As a non-partisan organization, the Society for Political Inquiries welcomed diverse opinions and showed that men from different sides of the political arena could come together for fruitful discussion.[15]

In May 1787 delegates from throughout the United States came to Philadelphia to attend the Constitutional Convention at Independence Hall. As they had during the Continental Congress, the Powels opened their doors and welcomed the delegates. Though politics fascinated Elizabeth Powel, her sisters wondered whether the male politicians appreciated her input. One sister wrote to another that in society Elizabeth would 'animate and give a brilliancy to the whole conversation' but commented, 'Her patriotism causes too much anxiety. Female politicians are always ridiculed by the other sex.'[16]

Franklin, who was elected a delegate to the Constitutional Convention to represent Pennsylvania, welcomed other delegates to Franklin Court. The convention was scheduled to begin on Monday 14 May, but the delegates from most states had yet to reach Philadelphia by then, preventing a quorum and delaying its start. Franklin accepted the delay with grace and hosted a party in the meantime. On 16 May delegates already in town gathered at Franklin Court for dinner. Having recently received a cask of porter from London brewer Thomas Jordan, Franklin could think of no better time to broach it. Writing Jordan a letter of thanks, Franklin described how his guests received the cask: 'Its contents met with the most cordial reception and universal approbation.' Jordan's Porter was the best the delegates had ever tasted.[17]

Ellicott called Franklin the 'Venerable Nestor of America', a label that seems especially appropriate to describe Franklin's role in the Constitutional Convention. Nestor was the ancient Greek king of

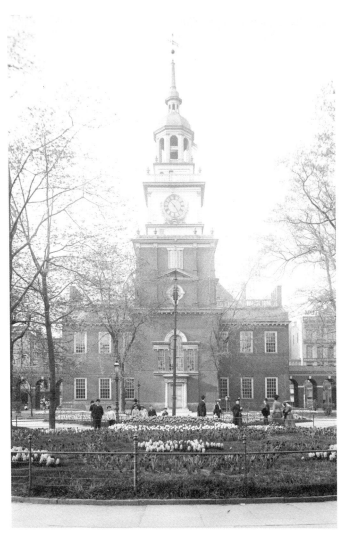

Independence Hall, Philadelphia, *c.* 1900, photograph.

Pylos who led his soldiers during the Trojan War and distinguished himself for his eloquence, justice, prudence and wisdom. After the war, Nestor enjoyed the peace and tranquillity due to his age and wisdom. As a young man, Franklin had quoted Pope's *Odyssey* to compare himself to Ulysses. Since the comparison to Nestor suits Franklin in old age, Pope's translation of Homer's *Iliad* may be a more fitting source for the last chapter of Franklin's life:

> To calm their passion with the words of age,
> Slow from his seat arose the Pylian sage;
> Th' experienc'd Nestor, in persuasion skill'd,
> Words, sweet as honey, from his lips distill'd.[18]

Not until Friday 25 May did the states reach a quorum and begin the Constitutional Convention. Washington was elected president of the convention. A hard rain prevented Franklin from attending the first day of the convention. He did not take his seat until Monday, but from then on, Franklin diligently attended every day for the next four months. He did not speak on the convention floor very often, but he coaxed others towards his point of view, using his charm and storytelling ability to help them see things more clearly.

On 4 June Franklin spoke against giving the national executive an absolute veto over the legislature, concerned that it would lead to an abuse of power akin to what Pennsylvania had experienced under the proprietary governors. An absolute executive veto could lead to monarchy, he observed. The convention unanimously agreed.

Towards the end of June, the convention approached the contentious issue of legislative representation. Delegates from the smaller states argued that every state should be equally represented in the legislature. The larger states argued that representation should be directly proportionate to each state's population. On 2 July Franklin was elected to a committee to settle the issue. He initially advocated proportionate representation in both houses, but the smaller states refused.

The larger states were willing to agree to equal representation in the Senate, provided representatives in the House were proportionate and that the House of Representatives controlled the spending bills. Debate over his scheme, which became known as the Great Compromise, lasted until 11 July. Franklin thought that giving the House of Representatives power over the spending bills made good sense and sought to persuade others. He ultimately persuaded enough to pass the measure. Franklin had kept the convention together at a crucial moment when the delegates were ready to break up and go home without forming a federal government.[19]

Throughout that summer convention, delegates and others visited Franklin Court. None left a fuller account than the Reverend Dr Manasseh Cutler, who came to Franklin Court with a prominent convention delegate from Massachusetts, Elbridge Gerry. They found Franklin seated in his octogenarian's garden in the shade.

He was entertaining some other guests with a recent addition to his cabinet of curiosities: a two-headed snake that had been caught outside Philadelphia. Talking about the snake as he showed it to his guests, Franklin wondered what would happen 'if it was traveling among bushes, and one head should choose to go on one side of the stem of a bush and the other head should prefer the other side, and that neither of the heads would consent to come back or give way to the other.' Franklin started to compare the snake's plight with the Constitutional Convention. Before he could develop his comparison any further, another delegate reminded him that the convention proceedings must be kept in strict secrecy, thus depriving Cutler, and posterity, of a great anecdote.[20]

After dark, Franklin invited his guests into the library. In his account, Cutler does not say precisely how they entered, but the passage was tricky. In the new wing of his home, it was impossible to go directly from the ground-floor dining room to the upper-floor library because Franklin had excluded a staircase, which would have taken too much space away from his books. To access the library, guests had to go through the main house. It was a little cumbersome, but Franklin liked going that way as he led guests to his library. The intricate passage added mystery and allure. They either went through a bed chamber, or they entered through one of the closets in the old drawing room.

Franklin showed them other curiosities, natural and man-made. That evening, most of the guests continued to talk politics, so Cutler, to his great delight, had their host to himself. Franklin, who could sense a guest's interests, would shape a tour of his library accordingly. Since Cutler's passion was botany, Franklin showed him some of his botanical works. That year, Franklin received a copy of Linnaeus's *Families of Plants*, a presentation copy from Erasmus Darwin, no less. Cutler spent the most time looking at Johann Sebastian Mueller's *Illustration of the Sexual System of Linnaeus*. Fothergill had given this huge folio to Franklin to present to the American Philosophical Society. It would eventually end up there, but Franklin held on to it for the time being and even inscribed it with his distinctive shelf mark.[21] Describing the experience, Cutler wrote,

> [This book] afforded me the greatest pleasure of any one thing in his library. It was a single volume, but so large that it was with great difficulty that the Doctor was able to raise it from a low shelf and lift it on to the table; but with that senile ambition common to old people, he insisted on doing it himself, and would permit no person to assist him, merely to show us how much strength he had remaining. It contained the whole of Linnaeus Systima Vegetabilia, with large cuts of every plant, and colored from nature. It was a feast to me, and the Doctor seemed to enjoy it as well as myself. We spent a couple of hours in examining this volume.[22]

On Friday 20 July, debate in the convention turned towards the issue of impeachment. A resolution had been introduced that included a clause allowing the national executive to be impeached and removed from office for malpractice or neglect of duty. Two delegates moved to strike that part of the resolution, arguing that the national executive should not be impeachable while in office. Their motion met vehement resistance.[23]

'If he be not impeachable whilst in office,' William Richardson Davie, a delegate from North Carolina, argued, 'he will spare no efforts or means whatever to get himself re-elected.'

'No point is of more importance than that the right of impeachment should be continued,' said George Mason, concurring with Davie. 'Shall the man who has practiced corruption and by that means procured his appointment in the first instance, be suffered to escape punishment, by repeating his guilt?'

Franklin agreed, arguing that impeachment would be the best way to punish the president when his misconduct should deserve it. It would also allow his acquittal should he be unjustly accused. Without an impeachment process built into the Constitution, Franklin argued, the only way to remove a corrupt president would be assassination.

James Madison agreed. He thought that an impeachment process should be built into the Constitution to defend against a corrupt, unprincipled or incompetent national executive. Madison listed several possible outcomes resulting from a corrupt national leader. Read in retrospect, Madison's words are bone-chilling. 'He might pervert his administration into a scheme of peculation or oppression. He might betray his trust to foreign powers,' Madison argued. 'In the case of the executive magistracy which was to be administered by a single man, loss of capacity or corruption was more within the compass of probable events, and either of them might be fatal to the republic.'

Charles Willson Peale,
James Madison, 1783,
watercolour on ivory.

Monday 17 September was the last day of the Constitutional Convention. The Constitution had been engrossed, and it was ready for the delegates to sign, though some remained unsure whether they should. After the Constitution was read, Franklin rose with a written speech, which he handed to fellow Pennsylvania delegate James Wilson to read. Franklin urged every member to 'doubt a little of his own infallibility', put aside specific reservations and vote to approve the Constitution.[24]

There is no telling how much Franklin's final speech convinced the delegates to sign the Constitution, but by the time they were through, only three refused to sign. When the delegates had almost finished signing, Franklin said something to the men near him, which one recorded for posterity:

Henry Hintermeister, *The Foundation of American Government*, *c.* 1925, photomechanical print after painting, depicting George Washington, Benjamin Franklin and others signing the U.S. Constitution in Philadelphia.

Whilst the last members were signing, Doctor Franklin, looking towards the President's chair, at the back of which a rising sun happened to be painted, observed to a few members near him, that painters had found it difficult to distinguish in their art, a rising, from a setting, sun. I have, said he, often and often, in the course of the session, and the vicissitudes of my hopes and fears as to its issue, looked at that behind the President, without being able to tell whether it was rising or setting: but now at length, I have the happiness to know, that it is a rising, and not a setting sun.[25]

Once the Constitutional Convention adjourned, the delegates went to City Tavern to dine together. After dinner, some ended up at the Powels' Third Street home, including Franklin and James McHenry, a delegate from Maryland, who recorded the episode. After enduring the secrecy of the convention proceedings all summer, Elizabeth Powel was eager to hear what the delegates had decided. No longer bound by secrecy, they could now talk freely about what had happened. This story has often been repeated, but much confusion surrounds it. One previously unrecorded version supplies additional detail and helps flesh it out.[26]

'Well, Doctor,' Elizabeth Powell asked when he entered their home, 'We are happy to see you abroad again: pray what have we got?'

'A republic, madam, if you can keep it,' Franklin told her.

'And why not keep a good thing', she asked, 'when we have got it?'

'Because madam', Franklin replied, 'there is in all republics a certain ingredient, of which the people having once tasted, think they can never get enough.'

The month before the Constitutional Convention began, Franklin had been elected president of the local anti-slavery organization. With the Constitution written and the convention adjourned, he could now devote his energy to abolition. The organization had originally been founded in 1775, but it languished during the Revolutionary War. It was reorganized in 1784, and, in 1787, a new constitution was adopted and it was renamed the Pennsylvania Society for Promoting the Abolition of Slavery, for the Relief of Free Negroes Unlawfully Held in Bondage, and for Improving the Condition of the African Race.

Shortly after Franklin was elected president of the society, Benjamin Rush enjoyed tea and conversation with him. Over the next few years, they would often get together and discuss a variety of topics. Slavery was one. Education was another. Franklin spoke freely about teaching Greek and Latin, which he called the quackery of literature. Less than a month after that conversation, Rush mentioned the subject in his correspondence with John Adams. Rush's words and imagery reflect his conversation with Franklin: 'Who are guilty of the greatest absurdity – the Chinese who press the feet into deformity by small shoes, or the Europeans

Charles B. J. Févret de Saint-Mémin, *Benjamin Rush*, 1802, engraving.

and Americans who press the brain into obliquity by Greek and Latin?'[27]

As they discussed slavery, Franklin recalled printing an early anti-slavery tract, Benjamin Lay's *All Slave-Keepers that Keep the Innocent in Bondage, Apostate*. Franklin recalled that the book 'though confused, contained just thoughts and good sense, but in a bad order'. Lay himself admitted that the work was not arranged very well, but, poor organization aside, *All Slave-Keepers* is a landmark in abolitionist thought, being one of the first direct calls to abolish slavery.[28]

Franklin's subsequent experience with the Bray Associates had fostered his anti-slavery feelings. Now, in his retirement, he could devote more effort to the cause. On behalf of the Pennsylvania Society for Promoting the Abolition of Slavery, Franklin petitioned Congress in February 1790 against slavery and the slave trade, urging Congress 'to countenance the restoration to liberty of those unhappy men, who, alone, in this land of freedom, are degraded into perpetual bondage'.[29]

The petition came up for discussion on the floor of Congress. James Jackson, a congressman from Georgia, spoke at length in an elaborate defence of slavery. His ignorant remarks inspired Franklin to write 'Sidi Mehemet Ibrahim on the Slave Trade', which satirized Jackson's defence of slavery. Written as a letter to the editor of the *Federal Gazette* and signed 'Historicus', this work gave Franklin a new opportunity to indulge his passion for hoaxes. Historicus, having read a speech in a seventeenth-century history of the Barbary Coast, presents it to the readers of the *Federal Gazette*, framing it to provide the historical context.[30]

Sidi Mehemet Ibrahim speaks in defence of the Muslim practice of enslaving Christians. His speech amounts to a paraphrase of the speech Jackson gave on the floor of Congress. It reveals Jackson's prejudice, hypocrisy and narrow-mindedness. William Lloyd Garrison, who would reprint Franklin's hoax in *The Liberator*, an abolitionist newspaper, remarked,

> Not a slave owner, probably, not a single excuser of the slave system, on perusing the speech of Sidi Mehemet Ibrahim, can be so blind as not to perceive himself represented in propria persona, as in a mirror, or so obtuse as not to comprehend the folly of his own logic.[31]

'Sidi Mehemet Ibrahim on the Slave Trade' would be Franklin's last public writing. The third week of April, he started having more and more difficulty breathing. Around eleven o'clock on the evening of 17 April 1790, Benjamin Franklin quietly expired. Though he had been afflicted with painful bladder stones for several years, his official cause of death was pleurisy, the pulmonary affliction that had almost taken his life as a young man. Polly Hewson, who had emigrated to Philadelphia with her three children, was present for Franklin's final moment. She informed a correspondent, 'I was faithful witness of the closing scene, which he sustained with that calm fortitude which characterized him through life.'[32]

Before his death. Franklin had added a codicil to his will, creating a philanthropic scheme guaranteed to last two hundred years. Franklin designed the scheme to encourage others to emulate the lifestyle he had exemplified. From the salary he had received as President of Pennsylvania, he left one thousand pounds sterling each to Boston and Philadelphia. Married men under 25 with good moral standing in the community, who had served their apprenticeships and now wished to establish businesses of their own could take out low-interest loans from the endowment. At the end of two hundred interest-accruing years, the funds would be given to each city.

The interest fell short of Franklin's estimate, largely due to mismanagement of funds, but on 17 April 1990, which marked the two-hundredth anniversary of his death, the Philadelphia fund amounted to over half a million dollars. As part of the bicentenary conference organized by Leo Lemay, a committee of scholars and city officials met to decide what to do with the Philadelphia fund. At a gala celebration inside Independence Hall, Mayor Wilson Goode announced that the fund would be used for education grants to award students who wished to learn crafts or trades.[33]

Franklin's last act of philanthropy seems motivated by the predominant impulse underlying his autobiography, which he left unfinished at the time of his death. Much as he promotes himself in the autobiography as a model of behaviour for his readers to emulate, he designed his final philanthropic scheme to reward young men who lived Franklin-like lives. The fund would help their businesses thrive and, ideally, let them become upstanding members of their community. Though Franklin wanted others to succeed, he did not want them to lose their compassion or their willingness to help others. Perhaps no one has done more to define the American way of life, nor has anyone better exemplified it. Benjamin Franklin is the heart of the American Dream.

References

Introduction

1 Mark Twain, 'The Late Benjamin Franklin', *Galaxy* (July 1870), p. 138.
2 Ibid., p. 139.
3 J. A. Leo Lemay, 'Benjamin Franklin and His Enemies', *Pennsylvania Magazine of History and Biography*, CXX/4 (October 1996), p. 374; Alan Gribben, *Mark Twain's Library: A Reconstruction* (Boston, MA, 1980), vol. I, p. 241.
4 Benjamin Franklin, 'Poor Richard Improved, 1758', in *The Papers of Benjamin Franklin*, ed. Leonard W. Labaree et al., 43 vols to date (New Haven, CT, 1959–), vol. VII, p. 341. In this and subsequent quotations from Franklin and other historical figures, capitalization has been modernized.
5 *The National Union Catalog Pre-1956 Imprints* (London, 1971), vol. CVXXXIII, pp. 132–4.
6 Michel Chevalier, *Society, Manners and Politics in the United States* (Boston, MA, 1839), pp. 200–201; Benjamin Franklin, 'The Way to Wealth', in *The Immortal Mentor: or, Man's Unerring Guide to a Healthy, Wealthy and Happy Life* (Cincinnati, OH, 1815), pp. 71–82.
7 M. G. Hubbard, *Saint-Simon: Sa vie et ses travaux* (Paris, 1857), p. 15.
8 Benjamin Franklin, *Conseils pour faire fortune* (Paris, 1848), p. [ii].
9 Honoré de Balzac, *Illusions perdues* (Paris, 1901), p. 128.
10 Lord Byron, 'Reply to *Blackwood's Edinburgh Magazine*', in *The Works*, ed. E. H. Coleridge and R. E. Prothero (London, 1905), vol. XI, p. 495.
11 Lord Byron, 'The Age of Bronze', in *Works*, vol. V, p. 554.
12 Leigh Hunt, *Lord Byron and Some of His Contemporaries* (London, 1828), vol. II, p. 184.
13 Stuart P. Sherman, 'What Is a Puritan?', *Atlantic Monthly*, CXXVIII/3 (September 1921), p. 353.
14 Leigh Hunt, *The Autobiography of Leigh Hunt* (New York, 1850), vol. I, p. 129.

15 [John Anster], 'Leigh Hunt', *Dublin University Magazine*, XXXVI/213 (September 1850), p. 273.

16 P. M. Zall, ed., *Ben Franklin Laughing: Anecdotes from Original Sources by and about Benjamin Franklin* (Berkeley, CA, 1980), no. 151.

17 'The First American Humorist', *Personal Efficiency* (April 1917), p. 16.

18 Stuart P. Sherman, 'Franklin', in *The Cambridge History of American Literature*, ed. William Peterfield Trent et al. (New York, 1917), vol. I, p. 91.

19 Albert Henry Smyth, ed., *The Writings of Benjamin Franklin* (New York, 1905–7), vol. I, p. 171.

20 Mark Hentemann, writer, 'The Splendid Source', *Family Guy* [TV programme], season 8, episode 19, aired 16 May 2010 on Fox, USA.

21 Quoted in Jacob Zeitlin and Homer Woodbridge, *Life and Letters of Stuart P. Sherman* (New York, 1929), vol. I, p. 264.

22 Sherman, 'Franklin', pp. 95, 108.

23 D. H. Lawrence, *Studies in Classic American Literature*, ed. Ezra Greenspan et al. (Cambridge, 2003), pp. 181–2.

24 Ibid., pp. 181, 185; Charles E. Robinson, ed., *The Frankenstein Notebooks* (New York, 1996), vol. I, p. lx.

25 Stuart P. Sherman, 'America Is Discovered', in *D. H. Lawrence: The Critical Heritage*, ed. Ronald P. Draper (London, 1970), pp. 208, 210.

26 Lawrence, *Studies*, p. 20.

27 Ibid., p. 21.

28 V. S. Pritchett, 'Books in General', *New Statesman and Nation* (27 September 1941), p. 309.

29 D. W. Brogan, 'The Pursuit of Happiness', *Spectator* (17 March 1939), p. 452.

30 Carl Van Doren, *Benjamin Franklin* (New York, 1938), p. 551; Zall, *Anecdotes*, no. 290.

31 'Anecdote', *Evening Post* (31 October 1836); Frederick Reynolds, *Life, A Comedy* [1801] (Philadelphia, PA, 1802), p. 43.

32 Malcolm Cowley, 'Tribute to Ben Franklin', *New Republic* (26 October 1938), p. 338.

33 Benjamin Franklin, 'Silence Dogood', in *Papers*, vol. I, p. 19.

34 Ibid., p. 27.

35 'Weekend Edition Sunday (National Public Radio), November 24, 1996', *Ancient Gonzo Wisdom: Interviews with Hunter S. Thompson*,

ed. Anita Thompson (New York, 2009), p. 194; Hunter S. Thompson, 'The Questionnaire', *The Guardian* (27 December 1997), p. B43; Hunter S. Thompson, *The Great Shark Hunt: Strange Tales from a Strange Time* (New York, 1979), p. 270.

36 Jorge Luis Borges, *Introducción a la literatura norteamericana* (Buenos Aires, 1967), p. 14; Hunter S. Thompson, *The Curse of Lono* (New York, 1983), p. 6; Kevin T. McEneaney, *Hunter S. Thompson: Fear, Loathing, and the Birth of Gonzo* (Lanham, MD, 2016), p. 176.

1 The Cabinet of Curiosities

1 Letter from Benjamin Franklin to Hans Sloane, 2 June 1725, in *The Papers of Benjamin Franklin*, ed. Leonard W. Labaree et al., 43 vols to date (New Haven, CT, 1959–), vol. I, p. 54.

2 Kevin J. Hayes, 'Benjamin Franklin, An American Satirist', in *Critical Insights: Satire*, ed. Robert C. Evans (New York, 2020), pp. 209–11.

3 Benjamin Franklin, *The Autobiography of Benjamin Franklin: A Genetic Text*, ed. J. A. Leo Lemay and P. M. Zall (Knoxville, TN, 1981), p. 42.

4 Ibid., p. 20.

5 Ibid., pp. 26, 36, 57.

6 J. A. Leo Lemay, *The Life of Benjamin Franklin*, 3 vols (Philadelphia, PA, 2006–9), vol. I, pp. 265–7.

7 'Advertisements', *American Weekly Mercury* (30 July 1724).

8 Lemay, *Life*, vol. I, p. 267.

9 'Advertisements', *Grub Street Journal* (15 March 1732).

10 William Stark, *The Works of the Late William Stark*, ed. James Carmichael Smyth (London, 1788), p. 92.

11 Kevin J. Hayes, *Shakespeare and the Making of America* (Stroud, 2020), pp. 49–50.

12 Franklin, *Autobiography*, p. 44.

13 Amy Louise Erikson, 'Mistresses and Marriage: or, A Short History of the Mrs', *History Workshop Journal*, 78 (Autumn 2014), p. 39.

14 Walter Isaacson, *Benjamin Franklin: An American Life* (New York, 2003), p. 44.

15 Amy Louise Erikson, 'Eleanor Mosley and Other Milliners in the City of London Companies, 1700–1750', *History Workshop Journal*, 71 (Spring 2011), p. 152.

16 Franklin, *Autobiography*, p. 44.

17 Ibid., p. 45.

18 James Delbourgo, 'When the Printer Met the Virtuoso', *Reviews in American History*, XXXVI/4 (December 2008), p. 485.

19 Zacharias Conrad von Uffenbach, 'Sloane's Museum at Bloomsbury [1710]', in *Sir Hans Sloane: Collector, Scientist, Antiquary, Founding Father of the British Museum*, ed. Arthur MacGregor (London, 1994), p. 30; John Pavin Phillips, 'Sir Hans Sloane at Home', *Notes and Queries*, 2nd ser., vol. XII (7 September 1861), p. 188.

20 Uffenbach, 'Sloane's Museum', p. 30.

21 Christian Heinrich Erndl, *The Relation of a Journey into England and Holland, in the Years, 1706, and 1707* (London, 1711), pp. 37–8.

22 Pehr Kalm, 'Sloane's Museum at Chelsea [1748]', trans. William R. Mead, in *Sir Hans Sloane*, ed. MacGregor, p. 32.

23 John Selden, *Table-Talk*, 3rd edn (London, 1716), p. 107.

24 Benjamin Franklin to Mary Stevenson, 13 September 1760, in *Papers*, vol. IX, pp. 212–13; P. M. Zall, ed., *Ben Franklin Laughing: Anecdotes from Original Sources by and about Benjamin Franklin* (Berkeley, CA, 1980), no. 10.

25 Phillips, 'Sir Hans', p. 188; Erndl, *Relation*, p. 38; Edwin Wolf, 2nd, and Kevin J. Hayes, *The Library of Benjamin Franklin* (Philadelphia, PA, 2006), p. 30.

26 Phillips, 'Sir Hans', p. 188; Uffenbach, 'Sloane's Museum', pp. 30–31.

27 Pehr Kalm, 'Speaking about Natural History, 1748', in *Franklin in His Own Time: A Biographical Chronicle of His Life, Drawn from Recollections, Interviews, and Memoirs by Family, Friends, and Associates*, ed. Kevin J. Hayes and Isabelle Bour (Iowa City, IA, 2011), p. 3.

28 Samuel Keimer, *A Brand Pluck'd from the Burning* (London, 1718), pp. 1, 8; Franklin, *Autobiography*, p. 27.

29 W. Sparrow Simpson, 'Lincoln's Inn Fields: The French Prophetess', *Notes and Queries*, 6th ser., vol. XI (10 January 1885), pp. 21–2.

30 Nick Bunker, *Young Benjamin Franklin: The Birth of Ingenuity* (New York, 2018), p. 187.

31 Kevin J. Hayes, *Herman Melville* (London, 2017), p. 112; 'Chelsea Pensioners', in *Around the World with Orson Welles* [1955], DVD (Chatsworth, CA, 1999).

32 *A Catalogue of the Rarities to be Seen at Don Saltero's Coffee-House in Chelsea* (London, 1731).

33 John Bunyan, *The Greatness of the Soul* (London, 1691), p. 27.

2 The Power of the Printed Word

1 Benjamin Franklin, 'Journal of a Voyage', in *The Papers of Benjamin Franklin*, ed. Leonard W. Labaree et al., 43 vols to date (New Haven, CT, 1959–), vol. I, p. 92.

2 Benjamin Franklin, 'Poor Richard Improved, 1748', in *Papers*, vol. III, p. 249.

3 Salem Pearse, *The Coelestial Diary: or, An Ephemeris for . . . 1726* (London, 1726), unpaginated.

4 James Dugan, 'Benjamin Franklin, Oceanographer', in *Men under Water*, ed. James Dugan and Richard Vahan (Philadelphia, PA, 1965), p. 5; Jacques Cousteau, *Man Re-enters the Sea* (New York, 1974), pp. 92–3.

5 Kevin J. Hayes, *Melville's Folk Roots* (Kent, OH, 1999), p. 4; Benjamin Franklin, 'Journal of a Voyage', in *Papers*, vol. I, p. 98.

6 Hannah Benner Roach, 'Benjamin Franklin Slept Here', *Pennsylvania Magazine of History and Biography*, LXXXIV/2 (April 1960), p. 135.

7 J. A. Leo Lemay, *Benjamin Franklin: A Documentary History* (Newark, DE, 1997).

8 *Every Man His Own Doctor: or, The Poor Planter's Physician*, 3rd edn (Philadelphia, PA, 1734), pp. 8–9.

9 Benjamin Franklin, *The Autobiography of Benjamin Franklin: A Genetic Text*, ed. J. A. Leo Lemay and P. M. Zall (Knoxville, TN, 1981), pp. 54–5.

10 Ibid., p. 62.

11 J. A. Leo Lemay, *The Life of Benjamin Franklin*, 3 vols (Philadelphia, PA, 2006–9), vol. I, p. 337; Whitfield J. Bell Jr, *Patriot-Improvers: Biographical Sketches of Members of the American Philosophical Society* (Philadelphia, PA, 1997), vol. I, pp. 11–15, 67.

12 Nicholas B. Wainright, 'Nicholas Scull's "Junto" Verses', *Pennsylvania Magazine of History and Biography*, LXXIII/1 (January 1949), pp. 82–4.

13 J. A. Leo Lemay, in discussion with the author, Lafayette, LA, 15 March 2002.

14 George W. Boudreau, 'Solving the Mystery of the Junto's Missing Member: John Jones, Shoemaker', *Pennsylvania Magazine of History and Biography*, CXXXI/3 (July 2007), p. 314.

15 [Joseph Breintnall], 'A Plain Description of One Single Street in This City', *American Weekly Mercury* (19 June 1729).

16 Ephraim Chambers, *Cyclopaedia: or, An Universal Dictionary of Arts and Sciences* (London, 1728), vol. I, pp. 31–2; Kevin J. Hayes, *The Library of John Montgomerie, Colonial Governor of New York and New Jersey* (Newark, DE, 2000), no. 122; Edwin Wolf, 2nd, *The Library of James Logan of Philadelphia, 1674–1751* (Philadelphia, 1974), no. 451; Benjamin Franklin, 'The Printer to the Reader', in *Papers*, vol. I, p. 158.

17 Chambers, *Cyclopaedia*, vol. I, p. 7; 'Abortion', *Universal Instructor in All Arts and Sciences: and Pennsylvania Gazette* (21 January 1729).

18 Benjamin Franklin, 'Martha Careful and Caelia Shortface', in *Papers*, vol. I, pp. 111–13.

19 Benjamin Franklin, 'The Busy-Body, No. 4', in *Papers*, vol. I, p. 125; Kevin J. Hayes, 'Benjamin Franklin', in *The Oxford Handbook of Early American Literature*, ed. Kevin J. Hayes (Oxford, 2008), pp. 434–5.

20 [Samuel Keimer], 'An Answer to the Busy-Body', *Universal Instructor* (13 March 1729).

21 Oswald Dykes, *Moral Reflexions upon Select British Proverbs* (London, 1708), p. 163.

22 Edwin Wolf, 2nd, and Kevin J. Hayes, *The Library of Benjamin Franklin* (Philadelphia, PA, 2006), no. 1849.

23 Though Chambers's *Cyclopaedia* is not listed in Wolf and Hayes, *Library of Benjamin Franklin*, Franklin's subsequent use of Chambers within the *Pennsylvania Gazette* clarifies that Samuel Keimer had included his copy of Chambers with his sale of the newspaper, ostensibly assuming that Franklin would want to continue his project of reprinting Chambers's work serially.

24 Benjamin Franklin, 'A Witch Trial at Mount Holly', in *Papers*, vol. I, p. 182; Francis B. Lee, 'Some Legal Allusions to Witchcraft in Colonial New Jersey', *New Jersey Law Journal*, XVII/6 (June 1894), p. 171.

25 Benjamin Franklin, 'Letter of the Drum', in *Writings*, ed. J. A. Leo Lemay (New York, 1987), p. 146.

26 Benjamin Franklin, 'Extracts from the *Gazette*, 1732', in *Papers*, vol. i, p. 274.

27 Franklin, *Autobiography*, p. 65.

28 Lemay, *Life*, vol. ii, p. 390; Franklin, *Autobiography*, p. 101.

29 Benjamin Franklin, 'Poor Richard, 1739', in *Papers*, vol. ii, pp. 217–18.

30 François Rabelais, *Pantagruel's Voyage to the Oracle of the Bottle: Being the Fourth and Fifth Books of the Works*, trans. Peter Motteux (London, 1694), p. 229.

31 Morris Palmer Tiley, *A Dictionary of the Proverbs in England in the Sixteenth and Seventeenth Centuries* (Ann Arbor, mi, 1950), no. F117; William Shakespeare, *Henry vi, Part 3*, v.6.11; Benjamin Franklin, 'Poor Richard Improved, 1751', in *Papers*, vol. iv, p. 88.

32 Benjamin Franklin, 'Old Mistresses Apologue', in *Papers*, vol. iii, p. 31.

33 Samuel Keimer, *A Brand Pluck'd from the Burning* (London, 1718), p. 54.

34 Franklin, *Autobiography*, p. 70.

35 Benjamin Franklin, 'To the Worshipfull, the Major, the Recorder, and the Rest of the Justices of the City of Philadelphia [3 January 1744]', *Collections of the Historical Society of Pennsylvania* (1853), vol. i, p. 268; John F. Watson, *Annals of Philadelphia* (Philadelphia, pa, 1830), p. 388; Benjamin Franklin, 'Extracts from the *Gazette*, 1731', in *Papers*, vol. i, p. 219.

36 Franklin, *Autobiography*, p. 80.

37 Lemay, *Life*, vol. ii, p. 6.

38 Ibid., pp. 7–8.

39 James N. Green, 'Peter Collinson, Benjamin Franklin, and The Library Company', *Annual Report of the Library Company of Philadelphia for the Year 2012* (Philadelphia, pa, 2013), p. 16.

40 Benjamin Franklin to the Abbé de La Roche, 29 March 1781, in *Papers*, vol. xxxiv, p. 496.

41 Lemay, *Life*, vol. ii, p. 89.

42 'Free or Accepted Masons', *Pennsylvania Gazette* (13 May 1731).

43 Benjamin Franklin, 'The Printer to the Reader', in *Papers*, vol. i, p. 158.

44 'At the Desire of Some of Our Country Subscribers', *Pennsylvania Gazette* (16 October 1729).

45 Lemay, *Life*, vol. ii, pp. 455–7.

3 The Improvement and Well-Peopling of the Colonies

1 J. A. Leo Lemay, *The Life of Benjamin Franklin*, 3 vols (Philadelphia, PA, 2006–9), vol. II, pp. 468–9; C. William Miller, *Benjamin Franklin's Philadelphia Printing, 1728–1766: A Descriptive Bibliography* (Philadelphia, PA, 1974), no. 349.

2 Benjamin Franklin, 'An Account of the New Invented Pennsylvania Fireplaces', in *The Papers of Benjamin Franklin*, ed. Leonard W. Labaree et al., 43 vols to date (New Haven, CT, 1959–), vol. II, p. 439.

3 Ibid., pp. 439–40; J. T. Desaguliers, *A Course of Experimental Philosophy*, vol. II (London, 1744), pp. 557–8; Edwin Wolf, 2nd, and Kevin J. Hayes, *The Library of Benjamin Franklin* (Philadelphia, PA, 2006), no. 846.

4 J. F. Gronovius to John Bartram, 2 June 1746, *The Correspondence of John Bartram, 1734–1777*, ed. Edmund Berkeley and Dorothy Smith Berkeley (Gainesville, FL, 1992), p. 278; Benjamin Franklin, *Beschreivinge van de nieuwe uitgevondene pensilvanische schoorsteenen* (Leyden, 1746); Benjamin Franklin to Cadwallader Colden, 16 October 1746, in *Papers*, vol. III, p. 92.

5 John Bartram to Benjamin Franklin, 29 July 1757, in *Papers*, vol. VII, p. 246; John Bartram to Peter Collinson, 30 May 1756, *Correspondence*, pp. 404–5.

6 'Mr John Bartram, Botanist', *Pennsylvania Gazette* (27 March 1746).

7 Lemay, *Life*, vol. II, pp. 487–8.

8 Benjamin Franklin, 'A Proposal for Promoting Useful Knowledge', in *Papers*, vol. II, p. 381.

9 John Bartram to Cadwallader Colden, 4 October 1745, *Correspondence*, p. 261.

10 Benjamin Franklin to Jared Eliot, 16 July 1747, in *Papers*, vol. III, p. 149.

11 Whitfield J. Bell Jr, '"All Clear Sunshine": New Letters of Franklin and Mary Stevenson Hewson', *Proceedings of the American Philosophical Society*, C/6 (17 December 1956), p. 521.

12 Benjamin Franklin to Cadwallader Colden, 16 October 1746, in *Papers*, vol. III, p. 92.

13 Alexander Pope, *An Essay on Man* (London, 1733), part I, lines 245–6.

14 J. A. Leo Lemay, 'Benjamin Franklin's Science', *New England Quarterly*, LXIV/1 (March 1991), p. 167; Benjamin Franklin, *Experiments and Observations on Electricity* (London, 1751), p. 12; Wolf and Hayes,

Library of Benjamin Franklin, no. 1184; Paul Leicester Ford, *Franklin Bibliography: A List of Books Written by, or Relating to Benjamin Franklin* (Brooklyn, NY, 1889), no. 77.

15 Franklin, *Experiments and Observations*, p. 35.

16 'At Henry Clark's', *Pennsylvania Gazette* (18 July 1745).

17 Quoted in John Jay Smith, *Recollections* (Philadelphia, PA, 1892), p. 228.

18 Benjamin Franklin, 'Colors of the Associator Companies', in *Papers*, vol. III, p. 268.

19 Quoted in *Papers*, vol. III, p. 186.

20 Lemay, *Life*, vol. II, p. 390; J. A. Leo Lemay, 'The Americanization of Benjamin Franklin', *Pennsylvania Magazine of History and Biography*, CXXX/2 (April 2006), p. 235.

21 James N. Green, 'English Books and Printing in the Age of Franklin', *The Colonial Book in the Atlantic World*, ed. Hugh Amory and David D. Hall (Cambridge, 2000), pp. 277–8.

22 Quoted in Kevin J. Hayes, 'The Board of Trade's "Cruel Sarcasm": A Neglected Franklin Source', *Early American Literature*, XXVIII/2 (1993), p. 173.

23 'The Following Letter Was Lately Publish'd in Virginia', *London Evening Post* (13 July 1751).

24 Benjamin Franklin, 'Rattlesnakes for Felons', in *Papers*, vol. IV, p. 133.

25 Benjamin Franklin to John Perkins, 13 August 1752, in *Papers*, vol. IV, p. 341; Lemay, *Life*, vol. III, p. 240.

26 Lemay, *Life*, vol. III, pp. 250, 258–60.

27 Benjamin Franklin, 'Constitutions of the Academy of Philadelphia', in *Papers*, vol. III, p. 421.

28 Whitfield J. Bell Jr, *Patriot-Improvers: Biographical Sketches of Members of the American Philosophical Society* (Philadelphia, PA, 1997), vol. I, p. 68.

29 Lemay, *Life*, vol. III, pp. 86–7.

30 Benjamin Franklin to Cadwallader Colden, 31 October 1751, in *Papers*, vol. IV, p. 202.

31 François Rabelais, *Pantagruel's Voyage to the Oracle of the Bottle: Being the Fourth of Fifth Books of the Works of Francis Rabelais*, trans. Peter Motteux (London, 1694), p. 175.

32 Joseph Priestley, 'Science, Religion, and Politics in London, 1769, 1795, 1802', in *Franklin in His Own Time: A Biographical Chronicle of His Life,*

Drawn from Recollections, Interviews, and Memoirs by Family, Friends, and Associates, ed. Kevin J. Hayes and Isabelle Bour (Iowa City, IA, 2011), pp. 40–42.

33 James A. Bear, ed., *Jefferson at Monticello* (Charlottesville, VA, 1967), pp. 3–4.

34 Wolf and Hayes, *Library of Benjamin Franklin*, no. 2314; *English Short-Title Catalogue*, no. T29595; Glyndwr Williams, 'Wigate, John, Naval Clerk', *Dictionary of Canadian Biography* (Toronto, 1974), vol. III, p. 663.

35 Lemay, *Life*, vol. III, pp. 315, 337.

36 Dr Alexander Hamilton, *Records of the Tuesday Club of Annapolis 1745–56*, ed. Elaine G. Breslaw (Urbana, IL, 1988), p. 447, and Dr Alexander Hamilton, *The History of the Ancient and Honorable Tuesday Club*, ed. Robert Micklus (Chapel Hill, NC, 1990), vol. III, pp. 214–15.

37 Hamilton, *History*, vol. I, pp. 330, 275.

38 Wolf and Hayes, *Library of Benjamin Franklin*, no. 973; J. B. Bordley, *Essays and Notes on Husbandry and Rural Affairs* (Philadelphia, PA, 1799), p. 613.

39 Daniel Royot, 'Benjamin Franklin as Founding Father of American Humor', *Reappraising Benjamin Franklin: A Bicentennial Perspective*, ed. J. A. Leo Lemay (Newark, DE, 1993), p. 394.

40 'Williamsburg, July 19', *Virginia Gazette* (19 July 1754).

41 Joseph Addison, *The Works*, ed. George Washington Greene (London, 1891), vol. I, pp. 187–8.

42 Benjamin Franklin to Peter Collinson, in *Papers*, vol. VI, p. 456.

43 Benjamin Franklin, 'Pennsylvania Assembly: Reply to the Governor', in *Papers*, vol. VI, p. 242.

44 Lemay, *Life*, vol. III, p. 522.

45 Benjamin Franklin, *The Autobiography of Benjamin Franklin: A Genetic Text*, ed. J. A. Leo Lemay and P. M. Zall (Knoxville, TN, 1981), p. 150.

4 An American Agent in London

1 Kevin J. Hayes, 'New Light on Peter and King, the Two Slaves Benjamin Franklin Brought to England', *Notes and Queries*, LX/2 (May 2013), pp. 205–9; Benjamin Franklin, 'An Address to the Public on Slavery',

in *The Writings of Benjamin Franklin*, ed. Albert Henry Smyth (New York, 1905–7), vol. x, p. 67.

2   Benjamin Franklin to William Brownrigg, 7 November 1773, in *The Papers of Benjamin Franklin*, ed. Leonard W. Labaree et al., 43 vols to date (New Haven, ct, 1959–), vol. xx, p. 465.

3   Benjamin Franklin, *The Autobiography of Benjamin Franklin: A Genetic Text*, ed. J. A. Leo Lemay and P. M. Zall (Knoxville, tn, 1981), pp. 163–5.

4   Ibid., p. 166; Benjamin Franklin to Deborah Franklin, 17 July 1757, in *Papers*, vol. vii, p. 243.

5   James N. Green, 'Peter Collinson, Benjamin Franklin, and The Library Company', in *The Annual Report of the Library Company of Philadelphia for the Year 2012* (Philadelphia, pa, 2013), p. 13.

6   George Simpson Eddy, 'Account Book of Benjamin Franklin Kept by Him During His First Mission to England as Provincial Agent, 1757–1762', *Pennsylvania Magazine of History and Biography*, lv/2 (1931), p. 102.

7   Franklin, *Autobiography*, pp. 126–7.

8   Ibid., pp. 166–7.

9   Benjamin Franklin to John Bartram, 11 January 1758, in *Papers*, vol. vii, p. 358; Benjamin Franklin, 'Supposition and Conjectures on the Aurora Borealis', in *Papers*, vol. xxviii, pp. 192–5.

10   [Richard Twiss], *Chess* (London, 1787), p. 190.

11   Benjamin Franklin to John Pringle, 21 December 1757, in *Papers*, vol. vii, p. 299.

12   Verner W. Crane, 'The Club of Honest Whigs: Friends of Science and Liberty', *William and Mary Quarterly*, xxiii/2 (April 1966), pp. 214–15; Edwin Wolf, 2nd, and Kevin J. Hayes, *The Library of Benjamin Franklin* (Philadelphia, pa, 2006), no. 2329.

13   James Boswell, *The Journal of James Boswell, 1769*, ed. Geoffrey Scott (London, 1930), p. 122; Josiah Quincy Jr, 'The London Journal, 1774–1775', in *Portrait of a Patriot: The Major Political and Legal Papers of Josiah Quincy, Junior*, ed. Daniel R. Coquillette and Neil Longley York (Boston, ma, 2007), vol. i, p. 244.

14   Robert Aspland, 'A Conversation with Franklin's London Friends, 1821', in *Franklin in His Own Time: A Biographical Chronicle of His Life, Drawn from Recollections, Interviews, and Memoirs by Family, Friends, and Associates*, ed. Kevin J. Hayes and Isabelle Bour (Iowa City, ia, 2011), p. 146.

15 John Densham to John Canton, 26 August 1769, in 'The Canton Papers', *Athenaeum* (17 February 1849), p. 163.

16 Benjamin Franklin, 'A Defense of the Americans', in *Writings*, ed. J. A. Leo Lemay (New York, 1987), pp. 518–30.

17 Benjamin Franklin, 'The Grand Leap of the Whale', in *Writings*, ed. Lemay, pp. 559–62.

18 [Daniel Defoe], *A Tour through the Whole Island of Great Britain*, 4th edn (London, 1748), vol. II, pp. 385–6.

19 Benjamin Franklin to Peter Franklin, 7 May 1760, in *Papers*, vol. IX, pp. 106–7.

20 Francis Hopkinson to Thomas Jefferson, 28 June 1786, in *Papers of Thomas Jefferson*, ed. Julian P. Boyd et al. (Princeton, NJ, 1950–), vol. X, p. 78.

21 Isaac Garrigues to Benjamin Franklin, 1762?, in *Papers*, vol. X, pp. 186–7.

22 Whitfield J. Bell Jr, *Patriot-Improvers: Biographical Sketches of Members of the American Philosophical Society: Volume One, 1743–1768* (Philadelphia, PA, 1997), pp. 224–5.

23 Peter Collinson to John Bartram, 25 July 1762, in *The Correspondence of John Bartram, 1734–1777*, ed. Edmund Berkeley and Dorothy Smith Berkeley (Gainesville, FL, 1992), p. 566.

24 Benjamin Franklin to John Waring, 17 December 1763, in *Religious Philanthropy and Colonial Slavery: The American Correspondence of the Associates of Dr. Bray, 1717–1777*, ed. John C. Van Horne (Urbana, IL, 1985), p. 204.

25 Benjamin Franklin, 'A Narrative of the Late Massacres', 30 January? 1764, in *Papers*, vol. XI, p. 55.

26 Deborah Franklin to Benjamin Franklin, 3 November 1765, in *Papers*, vol. XII, p. 350.

27 Benjamin Franklin to Samuel Rhoads, 8 July 1765, in *Papers*, vol. XII, p. 204; Samuel Butler, *The Genuine Remains in Verse and Prose*, ed. R. Thyer (London, 1759), vol. I, p. 38.

28 Benjamin Franklin to Charles Thomson, 11 July 1765, in *Papers*, vol. XII, p. 207; Kevin J. Hayes, *The Mind of a Patriot: Patrick Henry and the World of Ideas* (Charlottesville, VA, 2008), pp. 52–5.

29 House of Commons, 'Examination of Doctor Benjamin Franklin', in *Franklin in His Own Time*, ed. Hayes and Bour, p. 24.

30 Benjamin Franklin, 'The Frenchman and the Poker', in *Papers*, vol. XIII, p. 184.

31 Dixon Wecter, 'Francis Hopkinson and Benjamin Franklin', *American Literature*, XII/2 (May 1940), p. 201.

32 Benjamin Franklin, 'An Edict by the King of Prussia', 22 September 1773, in *Papers*, vol. XX, p. 418.

33 Linda Baumgarten, *What Clothes Reveal: The Language of Clothing in Colonial and Federal America* (New Haven, CT, 2002), p. 98.

34 Joseph Priestley, 'Science, Religion, and Politics in London, 1769, 1795, 1802', in *Franklin in His Own Time*, ed. Hayes and Bour, pp. 44–5.

5 The Declaration of Independence

1 John Adams, *Diary and Autobiography of John Adams*, ed. L. H. Butterfield et al. (Cambridge, MA, 1961), vol. II, p. 127.

2 Kevin J. Hayes, *Shakespeare and the Making of America* (Stroud, 2020), p. 189.

3 Thomas Coombe Jr to Benjamin Franklin, 24 September 1774, in *The Papers of Benjamin Franklin*, ed. Leonard W. Labaree et al., 43 vols to date (New Haven, CT, 1959–), vol. XXI, p. 316.

4 Benjamin Franklin, 'Journal of Negotiations in London', in *Papers*, vol. XXI, pp. 540–99, is the source for the ensuing story, which will not be documented separately.

5 Jonathan Shipley, *A Speech, Intended to Have Been Spoken on the Bill, for Altering the Charters of the Colony of Massachusett's Bay* (London, 1774), p. 14.

6 Benjamin Franklin to Lord Howe, 29 August 1776, in *Papers*, vol. XXII, p. 575.

7 Benjamin Franklin to Charles Thomson, 5 February 1775, in *Papers*, vol. XXI, p. 478.

8 Richard Bache to Benjamin Franklin, 24 December 1774, in *Papers*, vol. XXI, p. 401.

9 Joseph Priestley, 'Science, Religion, and Politics in London, 1769, 1795, 1802', in *Franklin in His Own Time: A Biographical Chronicle of His Life, Drawn from Recollections, Interviews, and Memoirs by Family, Friends, and Associates*, ed. Kevin J. Hayes and Isabelle Bour (Iowa City, IA, 2011), p. 43.

10 P. M. Zall, ed., *Ben Franklin Laughing: Anecdotes from Original Sources by and about Benjamin Franklin* (Berkeley, CA, 1980), p. 97.

11 Benjamin Franklin to David Hartley, 8 May 1775, and to Jonathan Shipley, 15 May 1775, in *Papers*, vol. XXII, pp. 34, 42.

12 Benjamin Franklin to Humphry Marshall, 23 May 1775, in *Papers*, vol. XXII, p. 51.

13 Henry James, *The American Scene* (New York, 1907), p. 281.

14 Carl Van Doren, *Benjamin Franklin* (New York, 1938), p. 534.

15 John Adams, 'Franklin as a Congressman and a Diplomat, 1775–1778', in *Franklin in His Own Time*, ed. Hayes and Bour, p. 53.

16 Benjamin Franklin to Richard Bache, 19 October 1775, in *Papers*, vol. XXII, pp. 241–2.

17 R. Howdell to John Coakley Lettsom, 12 January 1790, *Memoirs of the Life and Writings of John Coakley Lettsom*, ed. Thomas Joseph Pettigrew (London, 1817), vol. I, p. 175; Abigail Adams, 'Franklin in Boston and Paris, 1775 and 1784', in *Franklin in His Own Time*, ed. Hayes and Bour, p. 69.

18 Van Doren, *Benjamin Franklin*, p. 538.

19 Benjamin Franklin, 'Bradshaw's Epitaph', in *Writings*, ed. J. A. Leo Lemay (New York, 1987), p. 745.

20 Benjamin Franklin, 'The Rattlesnake as a Symbol of America', in *Writings*, ed. Lemay, pp. 745–6.

21 Thomas Paine, *Collected Writings*, ed. Eric Foner (New York, 1995), p. 25.

22 Kevin J. Hayes, *The Road to Monticello: The Life and Mind of Thomas Jefferson* (Oxford, 2008), p. 180.

23 Benjamin Franklin, 'Marginalia in *An Inquiry*', in *Papers*, vol. XVII, p. 346.

24 J. A. Leo Lemay, 'That Extraordinarily Busy Interval', *Pennsylvania Magazine of History and Biography*, CVII/1 (January 1983), p. 149.

25 Thomas Jefferson, 'Anecdotes of Doctor Franklin, 1818 and 1821', in *Franklin in His Own Time*, ed. Hayes and Bour, p. 136.

26 Benjamin Rush to John Adams, 20 July 1811, *Letters of Benjamin Rush*, ed. L. H. Butterfield (Princeton, NJ, 1951), vol. II, p. 1090.

27 Gordon S. Wood, *The Americanization of Benjamin Franklin* (New York, 2004), p. 165.

28 Benjamin Franklin to Lord Howe, 20 July 1776, in *Papers*, vol. XXII, p. 519.

29 Quoted in Jared Sparks, *Lives of John Ribault, Sebastian Rale, and William Palfrey* (Boston, MA, 1864), p. 415.

30 Adams, 'Franklin as a Congressman', p. 54.

31 Benjamin Franklin to Benjamin Rush, 14 July 1773, in *Papers*, vol. XX, p. 315.

32 Adams, 'Franklin as a Congressman', p. 56.

33 Quoted in Benjamin Rush to Julia Rush, 14 September 1776, *Letters of Benjamin Rush*, vol. I, p. 109.

6 An American Diplomat in Paris

1 Benjamin Franklin to Mary Hewson, 12 January 1777, and to Emma Thompson, 8 February 1777, in *The Papers of Benjamin Franklin*, ed. Leonard W. Labaree et al., 43 vols to date (New Haven, CT, 1959–), vol. XXIII, pp. 155, 298.

2 Theodore Hornberger, *Benjamin Franklin* (Minneapolis, MN, 1962), p. 41; *Fabulous Versailles* [DVD], dir. Sacha Guitry [1954] (Sandy Hook, CT, 2009); *Lafayette* [DVD], dir. Jean Dreville [1962] (Sandy Hook, CT, 2002).

3 Benjamin Franklin to Sarah Bache, 3 June 1779, in *Papers*, vol. XXIX, pp. 613; Jean Louise Henriette Campan, *Memoirs of the Private Life of Marie Antoinette* (New York, 1917), p. 211.

4 Carl Van Doren, *Benjamin Franklin* (New York, 1938), p. 580.

5 Benjamin Franklin, 'Dialogue between the Gout and Mr Franklin', in *Writings*, ed. J. A. Leo Lemay (New York, 1987), p. 948.

6 Abel Boyer, *Dictionnaire royal, françois-anglois et anglois-françois* (Paris, 1769), p. 79; Edwin Wolf, 2nd, and Kevin J. Hayes, *The Library of Benjamin Franklin* (Philadelphia, PA, 2006), no. 407.

7 Claude-Anne Lopez, *Mon Cher Papa: Franklin and the Ladies of Paris* (New Haven, CT, 1966), p. ii; Steve Martin, *The Pleasure of My Company: A Novel* (New York, 2003), pp. 45–6.

8 Quoted in Lopez, *Mon Cher Papa*, p. 151.

9 Benjamin Franklin to Jonathan Williams, 15 January 1781, in *Papers*, vol. XXXIV, p. 275.

10 Alfred Owen Aldridge, *Franklin and His French Contemporaries* (New York, 1957), p. 9.

11 Ibid., p. 10.

12 Pomponne Vincent to Benjamin Franklin, after 8 December 1778, in *Papers*, vol. xxviii, p. 208.

13 Claude-Anne Lopez, *My Life with Benjamin Franklin* (New Haven, ct, 2000), pp. 150–51.

14 William Weisberger, 'Benjamin Franklin: A Masonic Enlightener in Paris', *Pennsylvania History*, liii/3 (July 1986), p. 168.

15 John Adams, 'Franklin as a Congressman and a Diplomat, 1775–1778', in *Franklin in His Own Time: A Biographical Chronicle of His Life, Drawn from Recollections, Interviews, and Memoirs by Family, Friends, and Associates*, ed. Kevin J. Hayes and Isabelle Bour (Iowa City, ia, 2011), p. 65.

16 Lopez, *My Life*, pp. 152–3.

17 Benjamin Franklin, 'To the Royal Academy of [Brussels]', in *Writings*, ed. Lemay, p. 953.

18 Ibid., p. 954.

19 Kevin J. Hayes, 'Benjamin Franklin', *The Oxford Handbook of Early American Literature*, ed. Hayes (Oxford, 2008), p. 445.

20 Benjamin Franklin to George Washington, 5 March 1780, in *Papers*, vol. xxxii, p. 57.

21 Benjamin Franklin to Nathaniel Falconer, 28 July 1783, in *Papers*, vol. xl, p. 406.

22 Benjamin Franklin to Joseph Banks, 30 August 1783, in *Papers*, vol. xl, pp. 543–52.

23 P. M. Zall, ed., *Ben Franklin Laughing: Anecdotes from Original Sources by and about Benjamin Franklin* (Berkeley, ca, 1980), no. 98; J. A. Leo Lemay, 'Franklin, Benjamin', *American National Biography*, ed. John A. Garraty and Marc C. Carnes (Oxford, 1999), vol. viii, p. 392.

24 Stanley Finger, *Doctor Franklin's Medicine* (Philadelphia, pa, 2006), p. 225.

25 Pierre Jean Georges Cabanis, 'A Short Account of Benjamin Franklin, 1825', in *Franklin in His Own Time*, ed. Hayes and Bour, p. 159.

26 Benjamin Franklin, 'Information to Those Who Would Remove to America', in *Writings*, ed. Lemay, pp. 975–83; George Washington to Richard Henderson, 19 June 1788, in *The Papers of George Washington: Confederation Series*, ed. W. W. Abbot and Dorothy Twohig (Charlottesville, va, 1997), vol. vi, p. 341.

27 Lopez, *Mon Cher Papa*, p. viii; Zall, *Ben Franklin Laughing*, no. 170.

7 The Nestor of America

1 Benjamin Franklin to George Whatley, 23 May 1785, in *Writings*, ed. J. A. Leo Lemay (New York, 1987), pp. 1109–10.

2 Quoted in Kevin J. Hayes, *The Road to Monticello: The Life and Mind of Thomas Jefferson* (Oxford, 2008), p. 294.

3 Benjamin Franklin, 'Maritime Observations', in Albert Henry Smyth, ed., *The Writings of Benjamin Franklin* (New York, 1905–7), vol. IX, p. 381.

4 William Dampier, *A New Voyage Round the World*, 2nd edn (London, 1697), p. 412.

5 Franklin, 'Maritime Observations', p. 381.

6 Ibid., p. 413; Jonathan Williams, *Thermometrical Navigation* (Philadelphia, PA, 1799); John C. Fredriksen, 'Williams, Jonathan', *American National Biography*, ed. John A. Garraty and Marc C. Carnes (Oxford, 1999), vol. XXIII, p. 484.

7 'Smoky Chimneys', *Whitehall Evening-Post* (28 August 1787).

8 Wayne Craven, *Sculpture in America* (New York, 1968), p. 52.

9 Olive Moore Gambrill, 'John Beale Bordley and the Early Years of the Philadelphia Agricultural Society', *Pennsylvania Magazine of History and Biography*, LXVI/4 (October 1942), pp. 410–39; *Minutes of the Philadelphia Society for the Promotion of Agriculture from its Institution in February, 1785, to March, 1810* (Philadelphia, PA, 1854), p. 12.

10 Humphry Marshall, *Arbustrum Americanum: The American Grove* (Philadelphia, PA, 1785), pp. 49–50; Edwin Wolf, 2nd, and Kevin J. Hayes, *The Library of Benjamin Franklin* (Philadelphia, PA, 2006), no. 2198.

11 Keith Stewart Thomson, 'Benjamin Franklin's Lost Tree', *American Scientist*, LXXXVIII/3 (May–June 1990), pp. 203–6.

12 Andrew Ellicott, 'The Venerable Nestor of America, 1785', in *Franklin in His Own Time: A Biographical Chronicle of His Life, Drawn from Recollections, Interviews, and Memoirs by Family, Friends, and Associates*, ed. Kevin J. Hayes and Isabelle Bour (Iowa City, IA, 2011), p. 100.

13 Wolf and Hayes, *Library of Benjamin Franklin*, p. 19.

14 Benjamin Franklin to Marsilio Landriani, 14 October 1787, in *Writings*, ed. Smyth, vol. IX, p. 617.

15 Michael Vinson, 'The Society for Political Inquiries: The Limits of Republican Discourse in Philadelphia on the Eve of the Constitutional Convention', *Pennsylvania Magazine of History and Biography*, CXIII/2 (April 1989), pp. 188–9.

16 Anne J. Willing to Mary Willing Byrd, 19 March 1808, in Everard Kidder Meade, 'The Papers of Richard Evelyn Byrd I, of Frederick County, Virginia', *Virginia Magazine of History and Biography*, LIV/2 (April 1946), p. 117.

17 Benjamin Franklin to Thomas Jordan, 18 May 1787, in *Writings*, ed. Smyth, vol. IX, p. 582.

18 Alexander Pope, trans., *The Iliad of Homer* (London, 1715), p. 16.

19 Carl Van Doren, *Benjamin Franklin*, 1st edn [1938] (New York, 1991), pp. 749–50.

20 Manasseh Cutler, 'A Visit to Franklin Court, 1787', in *Franklin in His Own Time*, ed. Hayes and Bour, p. 113.

21 Wolf and Hayes, *Library of Benjamin Franklin*, nos. 2067, 2386.

22 Cutler, 'Visit', p. 114.

23 Max Farrand, ed., *The Records of the Federal Convention of 1787* (New Haven, CT, 1911), vol. II, pp. 64–6. The following speeches come from this source and will not be cited individually.

24 Benjamin Franklin, 'Franklin's Speech', in *The Documentary History of the Ratification of the Constitution*, ed. John P. Kaminski and Gaspare J. Saladino (Madison, WI, 1981), vol. XIII, p. 214.

25 James Madison, 'Franklin during the Constitutional Convention, 1787', in *Franklin in His Own Time*, ed. Hayes and Bour, p. 118.

26 [James McHenry], *The Three Patriots; or, The Cause and Cure of Present Evils* (Baltimore, MD, 1811), p. 6.

27 Benjamin Rush, 'The Wisdom and Experience of Mellow Old Age, 1785–1789, 1805, 1806', in *Franklin in His Own Time*, ed. Hayes and Bour, p. 105; Rush to John Adams, 21 July 1789, in *Letters of Benjamin Rush*, ed. L. H. Butterfield (Princeton, NJ, 1951), vol. I, p. 524.

28 Rush, 'Wisdom and Experience', p. 103; Marcus Rediker, *The Fearless Benjamin Lay: The Quaker Dwarf who Became the First Revolutionary Abolitionist* (Boston, MA, 2017), pp. 71–3.

29 Quoted in William Frederick Poole, *Anti-Slavery Opinions before the Year 1800* (Cincinnati, OH, 1873), p. 65.

30 Benjamin Franklin, 'Sidi Mehemet Ibrahim on the Slave Trade',
   in *Writings*, ed. Lemay, pp. 1157–60.

31 William Lloyd Garrison, 'A Mirror for Apologists', *The Liberator*
   (17 December 1831).

32 Mary (Polly) Stevenson Hewson, 'Closing Scenes of Dr Franklin's Life:
   In a Letter from an Eye-Witness', in *Franklin in His Own Time*,
   ed. Hayes and Bour, p. 120.

33 Michael E. Ruane, 'What Franklin Gave Us', *Philadelphia Inquirer*
   (19 April 1990), p. D01.

Select Bibliography

Notable Editions of Benjamin Franklin's Writings

Bigelow, John, ed., *The Complete Works of Benjamin Franklin*, 10 vols
    (New York, 1887–8)
Duane, William, ed., *The Works of Dr Benjamin Franklin*, 6 vols
    (Philadelphia, PA, 1808–18)
Franklin, William Temple, ed., *Memoirs of the Life and Writings of Benjamin
    Franklin, L.L.D.* (London, 1817–18)
Labaree, Leonard W., et al., eds, *The Papers of Benjamin Franklin*, 43 vols to
    date (New Haven, CT, 1959–)
Lemay, J. A. Leo, ed., *Writings* (New York, 1987)
——, and P. M. Zall, eds, *The Autobiography of Benjamin Franklin: A Genetic
    Text* (Knoxville, TN, 1981)
Smyth, Albert H., ed., *The Writings of Benjamin Franklin*, 10 vols (New York,
    1905–7)
Sparks, Jared, ed., *The Works of Benjamin Franklin*, 10 vols (Boston, MA,
    1836–40)

Reference Works

Buxbaum, Melvin H., *Benjamin Franklin: A Reference Guide, 1721[–83]*, 2 vols
    (Boston, MA, 1983–8)
Ford, Paul Leicester, *Franklin Bibliography: A List of Books Written by, or
    Relating to Benjamin Franklin* (New York, 1889)
Hayes, Kevin J., and Isabelle Bour, eds, *Franklin in His Own Time:
    A Biographical Chronicle of His Life, Drawn from Recollections,
    Interviews, and Memoirs by Family, Friends, and Associates* (Iowa City,
    IA, 2011)

Lemay, J. A. Leo, *The Canon of Benjamin Franklin, 1722–1776: New Attributions and Reconsiderations* (Newark, DE, 1986)

Miller, C. William, *Benjamin Franklin's Philadelphia Printing, 1728–1766: A Descriptive Bibliography* (Philadelphia, PA, 1974)

Wolf, Edwin, 2nd, and Kevin J. Hayes, *The Library of Benjamin Franklin* (Philadelphia, PA, 2006)

Zall, P. M., ed., *Ben Franklin Laughing: Anecdotes from Original Sources by and about Benjamin Franklin* (Berkeley, CA, 1980)

Biographical, Critical and Historical Studies

Aldridge, Alfred Owen, *Benjamin Franklin, Philosopher and Man* (Philadelphia, PA, 1965)

——, *Benjamin Franklin and Nature's God* (Durham, NC, 1967)

——, *Franklin and His French Contemporaries* (New York, 1957)

Anderson, Douglas, *The Radical Enlightenments of Benjamin Franklin* (Baltimore, MD, 1997)

Bunker, Nick, *Young Benjamin Franklin: The Birth of Ingenuity* (New York, 2018)

Carr, William G., *The Oldest Delegate: Franklin in the Constitutional Convention* (Newark, DE, 1990)

Chaplin, Joyce E., *The First Scientific American: Benjamin Franklin and the Pursuit of Genius* (New York, 2006)

Cohen, I. Bernard, *Benjamin Franklin's Science* (Cambridge, MA, 1990)

Crane, Verner W., *Benjamin Franklin and a Rising People* (Boston, MA, 1954)

Finger, Stanley, *Doctor Franklin's Medicine* (Philadelphia, PA, 2006)

Frasca, Ralph, *Benjamin Franklin's Printing Network: Disseminating Virtue in Early America* (Columbia, MO, 2006)

Granger, Bruce Ingham, *Benjamin Franklin: An American Man of Letters* (Ithaca, NY, 1964)

Green, James N., and Peter Stallybrass, *Benjamin Franklin: Writer and Printer* (London, 2006)

Hayes, Kevin J., ed., *Benjamin Franklin* (New York, 2008)

Lemay, J. A. Leo, *The Life of Benjamin Franklin*, 3 vols (Philadelphia, PA, 2006–9)

——, ed., *The Oldest Revolutionary: Essays on Benjamin Franklin* (Philadelphia, PA, 1976)

——, ed., *Reappraising Benjamin Franklin: A Bicentennial Perspective* (Newark, DE, 1993)

Lopez, Claude-Anne, *Mon Cher Papa: Franklin and the Ladies of Paris* (New Haven, CT, 1966)

——, *My Life with Benjamin Franklin* (New Haven, CT, 2000)

Lopez, Claude-Anne, and Eugenia W. Herbert, *The Private Franklin: The Man and His Family* (New York, 1975)

Middlekauff, Robert, *Benjamin Franklin and His Enemies* (Berkeley, CA, 1996)

Mulford, Carla, ed., *The Cambridge Companion to Benjamin Franklin* (Cambridge, 2008)

Pangle, Lorraine Smith, *The Political Philosophy of Benjamin Franklin* (Baltimore, MD, 2007)

Pasles, Paul C., *Benjamin Franklin's Numbers: An Unsung Mathematical Odyssey* (Princeton, NJ, 2008)

Schiff, Stacy, *A Great Improvisation: Franklin, France, and the Birth of America* (New York, 2005)

Talbott, Page, ed., *Benjamin Franklin: In Search of a Better World* (New Haven, CT, 2005)

Van Doren, Carl, *Benjamin Franklin* (New York, 1938)

Waldstreicher, David, *Runaway America: Benjamin Franklin, Slavery, and the American Revolution* (New York, 2004)

Acknowledgements

Reaktion's Critical Lives have become an important part of my writing life, thanks in no small part to Michael R. Leaman, who invited me to write a book about Edgar Allan Poe for the series a dozen years ago. Since then, he has graciously let me contribute additional volumes on Herman Melville, Mark Twain and now Benjamin Franklin. But the series is important to me not only as a writer, but as a reader. I have filled nearly an entire shelf with Critical Lives, and other contributors to the series have given me numerous ideas for mine. For *Pablo Picasso*, Mary Ann Caws concentrates on the *bande à Picasso* – that is, the close-knit group of friends who surrounded him. A similar approach works well with Franklin.

In graduate school at the University of Delaware, I was fortunate to study with J. A. Leo Lemay, the greatest Franklin scholar of his generation. After his death in 2008, I returned to Delaware for his memorial service. At the reception, following the service, I spoke with Wayne Craven, my art history professor and one of Leo's best friends. I told him, 'After my parents, no one has influenced me more than Leo Lemay.' What I said startled me a moment. I had never articulated my intellectual debt to Leo in that way, but as I mulled it over, I could not disagree with what I had told Wayne.

While researching *Jefferson in His Own Time*, I happily received a fellowship from the Robert H. Smith International Center for Jefferson Studies. This fellowship is the gift that keeps on giving. As one benefit, the Smith Center gave me off-site access to its online databases, which has proven to be a lifeline, since I have mostly written this book from home during a long period of self-quarantine while death and disease have swirled around the house. This project has let me use much material I had left unused from previous Franklin research at the Library Company of Philadelphia and the American Philosophical Society, two other institutions that deserve my heartfelt thanks.

Several individuals earned my thanks, as well. I have benefitted from my conversations about Franklin with A. Owen Aldridge, the greatest Franklin scholar of his generation. Lemay's teacher at the University of Maryland, Aldridge is my scholarly grandfather. His work reminds me of the importance of academic genealogy. At the Library Company of Philadelphia, John Van Horne gave me opportunities, ideas and encouragement. Most importantly, he gave me the opportunity to complete the work of his predecessor Edwin Wolf, 2nd, who devoted much of his career to reconstructing the library of Benjamin Franklin. I also thank Amy Erickson, whose study of women's life and work in eighteenth-century London has given me a new perspective on the mysterious Mrs T. As always, my wife Sooki has provided unceasing support and encouragement throughout the composition of this work. Tom Barden, my undergraduate teacher at the University of Toledo and now my neighbour, first got me thinking about the relationship between folklore and literature. To him this book is dedicated.

Photo Acknowledgements

The author and publishers wish to express their thanks to the below
sources of illustrative material and/or permission to reproduce it. Some
locations of artworks are also given below, in the interest of brevity:

The Diplomatic Reception Rooms, U.S. Department of State, Washington,
DC: p. 93; The John Work Garrett Library, The Sheridan Libraries,
Johns Hopkins University, Baltimore, MD: p. 81; Library of Congress,
Manuscript Division, Washington, DC: p. 164; Library of Congress, Prints
and Photographs Division, Washington, DC: pp. 6, 47, 75, 78, 85, 103,
118, 128 (Massachusetts Historical Society, Boston), 135, 146, 158, 171, 176,
177; The Metropolitan Museum of Art, New York: pp. 64, 66; Musée des
Beaux-Arts, Reims: p. 149; Musée Carnavalet, Histoire de Paris: p. 150;
National Galleries of Scotland, Edinburgh: p. 113; National Gallery of Art,
Washington, DC: pp. 127, 165, 179; National Portrait Gallery, Smithsonian
Institution, Washington, DC: pp. 130, 131; The New York Public Library:
pp. 110, 137, 142; Phillips Library, Peabody Essex Museum, Salem, MA (CC
BY 4.0): p. 65; photo Tonamel (CC BY 2.0): p. 102; Yale Center for British Art,
Paul Mellon Collection, New Haven, CT: pp. 25, 116.